D1714488

0

Embers of the Past

A historical novel

about

Poland,

Russia,

Revolution

family,

and

religion

by

Daniel Kavetsky

1

Cover design by:

Purpose on Paper
- Book Covers

Special Thanks to:

Angelica Hagman for
her support and
encouragement

Table Content

Dedication

Mieczyslaw Kawecki   1852-1921

Tatiana Podlesney   1878-1969

Tamara Medvededeff 1898-1986

Modest Kawecki   1899-1918

Valerjan Kavetsky   1902-1988

In the end all wars are civil wars because all men are brothers. -Francis Fenelon

Chapter 1

Karecki Family Estate, Tsar's Russia, Summer 1909

The mid-morning sun floods the bedroom, persuading a young girl to throw back the covers and visit the chamber pot. Chirping birds greet ten-year-old Krystyna Karecki, who splashes water on her face and opens wide the window, breathing in a cool spring breeze which dries her face. Looking toward the distant hills she thinks of her mother. *I cannot believe she left. Damn her.* The horse and rider draw her attention to the landscape below *That sounds like Midnight.* She delights at the sight of the stable boy leading the shiny black stallion to the carriage house. Chickens squawk as she hurls an apple down the lane. Mission accomplished. The boy turns. Cupping her mouth, she calls out, "Anatoly, meet me at the barn in ten minutes.

"As you wish, my lady."

How long can I keep devious meetings secret? the daughter of Czeslaw Karecki wonders. After slipping into a peasant-style cotton skirt and blouse she covers her curls with a babushka and stares mindlessly at the image in the mirror. Tears blurring her vision. From her dressing table, she pockets a lacquered candy tin, and tiptoes down the grand staircase and out the front door. The parading peacocks scurry away as she jumps on her bike, and coasts down the muddy lane to meet him.

Before Anatoly can greet his friend, she twists his arm and digs her fingernails into his wrist. "Get inside. No one can see us."

"What is wrong with you?" he protests, as he wipes blood on his trousers.

"I think my parents are getting a divorce," she screams, doubling over and holding her stomach.

Divorce? What do you mean?" Anatoly asks.

"Are you mocking me? I have a right to slap you," She attacks a hay bale instead, sinks to the ground and buries her reddened face in her hands.

"What did I do? Please, take a few deep breaths and count to ten. Get ahold of yourself."

"Maybe you are just ignorant of the word. Sometimes grownups decide living together is no longer possible. Why do I even talk to you?"

Anatoly hangs his head, raking his curly black hair with dirty fingernails. "Sorry, just trying to help," he reaches out to lift her from the dust and filth. Krystyna rejects the helping hand.

Clenching her fists, she pushes past him and sinks onto a hay bale. A breath of stale farm air gags her. She pulls her knees to herself and leans heavily against splintered wood, which rends her blouse and rips her skin. She stiffens against the pain.

"I know about your parents. While gardening, I sometimes heard them arguing, usually about religion or politics."

"You must promise to respect me always. If you call me 'Foxtail' again my brother will do more than pelt you with green chestnuts. Now sit next to me and just listen." Loosening the grip on herself, she continued, "Yesterday, my mother left. She was sitting on the portico between two large suitcases. When our eyes met, tears flowed so freely, it was hard to see or talk. She hugged me for the longest time. I sat on her lap, and she played with my curls. Then her parents picked her up. I never believed something like this could happen."

"You see, I can listen. You can talk to me anytime you want."

"We will see about that. But not today for sure."

"How about a smoke. It could help us relax and make peace. Did you bring a cigarette?"

She pulls the candy tin from her pocket. "I stole one and some matches,"

Anatoly smiles, lights the cigarette, and hands it to her. Krystyna laughs while inhaling, causing her to cough. One errant ember hits the ground. Soon smells like burnt biscuits and flashes of light jolt the pair into action. She runs for water while he beats the blaze with a horse blanket.

"Fire! Fire!" Krystyna calls. "We need water." Peasants arrive swiftly with bushels of well-water, dousing leaping flames. Thick dirty air darkens the barn.

The Lord of the Manor sniffs smoke drifting through his bedroom window. Billowing black soot blots the clear blue sky like an exclamation point. "What in God's name," he mutters as he throws back the covers, grabs his hickory cane, and struggles down the grand staircase, limping his way to the barn. "Someone will pay for this," he vows.

The children hide in the crowd but are soon confronted. "You, Anatoly, are a bad influence on my daughter. Thirty bales of hay gone and a singed barn. How can I keep you around? No pay for three months. You are on probation. I forbid you to have contact with Krystyna. Midnight did not kick over a lantern. You are a lying rascal. Go before my kind heart turns to stone."

"As you wish, sir," answers Anatoly, bowing profoundly and clicking his heels. "I am embarrassed and ashamed of my actions. I will find a

10

way to make amends." Avoiding Krystyna's gaze, he quietly exits.

"Krystyna, you are out of control. You are on house arrest until you prove yourself obedient. I see a boarding school in your future."

Boarding school? thought she. *He will work me to the bone now that mother is gone.* She climbed the stairs, accepting confinement in her room. *How can things disintegrate to such a state in less than twenty-four hours? Maybe when Igor and Konrad come home we can figure out how to survive in this fractured family.*

Chapter 2

No one was smiling when, some days later, Czeslaw summoned Krystyna, Konrad, one year her junior, and seven-year-old Igor to the drawing room. With her chin up and shoulders rolled back, she marched to the straight-back couch with a scowl on her face. Following her were her stiff-necked brothers, still wearing their military-school uniforms. Already in the room was Fr. Sazanov from the local Russian Orthodox monastery and Fr. Pulaski, SJ, Catholic priest from Riga. Czeslaw closed the French doors at opposite ends of the room. He invites each priest to offer an opening prayer, which they do competitively, using their own solemn language.

Czeslaw rises from his over-stuffed chair and walks to his mahogany desk. "Children, these papers represent a legal separation between your mother and me. It has taken several months to work out the details, but this agreement has been signed by your parents, your grandparents, the witnesses here, and the local constable. Contrary to callous rumors, your mother and I are not divorced. Religious law forbids it. Divorce can only be granted in rare cases by the head of the Church, that is, by Tsar Nicolas II himself. The provisions listed here, we pray, are in your best interests. You will live here during the summers but continue your education in boarding schools. Krystyna, your school is in Vilnius. I agree not to pursue baptism in the Catholic church for you currently. When you are of age you will make your own decisions about religion. This private arrangement must not be talked about in public. You will have the opportunity to see your mother at your grandparent's home on a limited basis. Now, my children, do you have any questions? "

So, you are saying we can stay in our Polish schools, but without the sacraments?" asks Igor.

"Well stated, Igor." Czeslaw presses on the arms of the chair to get up. He begins pacing the room, hands clasped behind his back. "Your mother and I have not been happy in our marriage for some time. The fault is ours, not yours. I hope that someday you can understand."

With that the adults retire to the parlor, taking their legal papers with them. The children sit silently, staring off into space in shock.

Finally, Konrad speaks up, "I'm numb like a frozen herring packed in ice. My feelings are unknown to me. All I know is words are getting caught in my throat. I hate my grandparents. It seems they are always stirring up trouble."

"I am not surprised. Mother has not been herself for a while now," suggests Igor. "She hardly came out of her room. I don't want to think about it. Let us go play some croquet."

"A good idea," exclaims Krystyna as she jumps up to fetch the mallets. She hurls them out an open window with all her might. "Last one out is a rotten egg," she cries, dashing out the back door before the tears wetting her face could be seen.

Chapter 3

Near the Eastern Front, Imperial Russia, August 1915

Ping-pong- ping! Marble-sized hail ricochets off the metal doors and roof as a train pulls into the station. "Wake up, young lady," whispers the old peasant woman as she lifts the head of the schoolgirl off her lap.

Coughing out steam, smoke, and bad air that smells like dung-soaked farmland, sixteen-year-old Krystyna Karecki sits up straight—screeching brakes jolt away her dreams. A beam of morning light illuminates the scene; miserable people sprawled across the floor like fallen chess pieces. Rubbing sleep from her irritated eyes, she asks, "*Babushka,* where are we.? Our rest-stop. If Vilnius is your destination, we part ways here."

Outside, thousands of refugees trudge along muddy roads, sinking deeper in the tracks on their way to central Russia. Some desperate souls make a frantic but futile run to board the slowing train.

"You are most kind. My name is Krystyna. I am finishing high school in Vilnius. I've made this trip before but never seen such chaos."

"I am Ludmilla. Yes, Latvia, my homeland, now belongs to the Germans. Russia gave up the territory, running like scared rabbits. It is costing them dearly. The occupiers have shut down mills and factories. I am from Rezekne, where I was working as a seamstress, making Russian uniforms. Now the plant supplies the German army with long-johns and fur headgear. Krystyna, look over there. Those soldiers in the crisp blue uniforms carrying long rifles. They are Latvian's Rifle brigade, Germany's most formidable foe on the eastern front.

My husband and my two boys serve with them."

"I've heard of them. Patriotic fighters. I come from Sebezh province, not far from your border."

The train whistles to a stop. "Attention, attention!" barks the station guard. "Those needing to relieve themselves use the trees. Women and children to the left. Men to the right.

So sorry, but our outhouses are overflowing." One gentleman in a breasted suit and tie and sporting a crisp fedora pleads, "Is anyone selling newspapers?"

The station guard answered, "No sir, but if you search the underbrush, you might find a flier, urging our boys to surrender. There were thousands of them, dropped from a German zeppelin a few days ago."

"Thank you. I will put several to good use."

"We part ways here," says Ludmilla as she sinks to the platform, pulling her bulky bundle with her.

"Thank you again, Ludmilla. Safe journey. You and your family will be in my thoughts and prayers until this unholy war is over."

The next day Krystyna is greeted by a dozen classmates and their driver at the Vilnius train station. She is smothered by the long arms of her best friend, Janina Ostrowski. Her friend's glasses bounce off the pavement. "Darn, how awkward of me," she says, picking them from the cobblestone and checking for scratches. "You look tired, my friend, but more beautiful than ever, with your sun-bleached chestnut hair and glowing suntan. Turn around. A French braid. How *au courant.* I love it. If only we could get rid of these boring school uniforms. But I have some bittersweet news for you. I'll tell you later."

"By no means Janina. There can be no secrets between us, even for a minute."

"Have it your way then. My aunt obtained a teaching position at the Academy of Arts in Krakow. So, I am an orphan again."

"Your Aunt Lucia is a very lovely person. And a very gifted painter. You will surely miss her. But what about your education?

"I am now a full-time boarding student." The duo take time to embrace and wipe away each other's tears.

"Let us make the best of a bad situation. You must take my side during pillow fights and other mischiefs. We have so much to talk about."

After a while the giggling schoolgirls climb into the back of the motor lorry for a short ride through town and up the winding drive to the convent on the hill. Russian troops parade in precise formations on cobbled streets below. Their faces betray fear, hunger, and fatigue.

Mother Superior greets the group as the lorry pulls into the *porte covert.* "Your lunch is ready, *Czernina* and black bread. After lunch, Janina, you can help your friend unpack and learn the house rules. The rest of you girls go the common room for the study period."

"Janina, there's something I need to tell you," Krystyna says in a lowered voice. "I had an argument with my father, *"You cannot go back to school at a time like this. I forbid it."*

"But this is my last year, and I have friends. You have no idea how tired I am of farm work. Managing the peasants is nearly impossible and stressful. Hard to stop them from stealing our produce and livestock. They think they are entitled to everything."

"If you leave, you are no daughter of mine."

"I told him I had plans which didn't include milking cows. At that point, I thought he would strike me, but he held his temper."

"I'm confused," Janina admitted. "What are your plans besides graduating?

"I want to travel, see the big city lights. Seek my fortune and fame."

"That is a red herring if I ever heard one. I know you better than that. You must tell me more."

"This is neither the time nor the place my sweet."

They enter the barren third-floor dormitory. On her bed is a school uniform, a nightgown, towel, and toothbrush. "Another uniform in your footlocker and the winter clothes," says Janina. "Let me see what you packed into that suitcase."

"Leather ankle boots, straight from Paris. One pair for you and a matching pair for me."

"I am truly grateful. Thank you so much. We are fortunate to be in this peaceful place, away from war, blood, and death."

"I agree," says Krystyna. "These are less then hopeful times."

***

Chapter 4

About a month later, Superior Sister Faustina's prayer efforts are interrupted by a persistent pounding on the heavy Convent doors. Sound waves echoed through the cloister walk and up the stairs to the chapel. On the cobbled streets below, the rhythmic cadence of goose-stepping soldiers rattles the sun-lit stained-glass windows. The Mother Superior stands, stiff and immobile, like a chapel statue. *Dear Lord, I never imagined the war would invade this peaceful place.* She wipes the dampness from her forehead while fumbling for a letter in her breast pocket. *"Lord, I need your help to suppress my anger. Are we really being evicted? This situation is crushing me.*

"Good morning General Von Krausmann. Forgive my weak German. I received your letter yesterday. We are shocked that the Russians abandoned us so quickly but grateful at the same time. No blood on our streets. How did you do it?"

"They didn't put up much of a fight. Strategic repositioning it's called. All you Poles and Jews will have to fend for yourselves."

"Before I show you around, I need a cold drink of water. Why is it again that you choose our school and convent over all the other religious properties in Vilnius?"

"Your location high on this hill suits us, an ideal spot to police the city. Our officers can also plan war strategies from here."

"So, you will put us out on the street? Sixteen nuns and dozens of schoolgirls? Some of our boarding students have just arrived. Have you no heart?"

"I don't know about that, Sister, but our needs are immediate. I will grant you refuge in your beloved chapel. But you must be gone by the end of the month. Mother, it's nothing personal. We need your buildings, that's all."

"But what will become of us? Homeless Polish girls and aged nuns. St. Joan of Arc pray for us. France could use her army about now."

"War has a way of changing things. Your problem is not mine, Reverend Mother. If your God exists, you'll find a way. Auf *Wiedersehen und veil Gluck.*"

Mother Faustina gathers all the nuns and students in the Chapel. "We are living in this sacred space for a while. You'll be sleeping on the pews, nuns on the right, and students on the left. We will gather around the altar for Mass and prayers. Thank God for His mercy. His ways are not ours, but we shall survive." Mother Superior works out an elaborate plan to move the whole operation to Riga, Russia's last stronghold on the Baltic. "We will merge with the orphanage run by the little Felician sisters. The good sisters are making the third floor available to us. Trust in Divine Providence. Whether we live or die, we belong to the Lord. I'll post schedules: classes, chapel, meals, kitchen duty, bedtimes, manual labor, and the like. I'm sending out permission letters."

Krystyna clutches her stomach and stretches her neck and shoulders. "Mother, may I see you?" she asked in a pleading voice.

"Meet me in the sacristy after Rosary. Today we pray the Sorrowful Mysteries."

Kristina squirms and shifts from one knee to the other and fidgets with her beads as she considers Jesus' Agony in the Garden. *"What anguish is in store for me if I'm found out."*

She hesitates before entering Mother's makeshift office. "Please check the address of my father. He is ill and staying with my Aunt Jadwiga. I have her address in my footlocker."

Kristina's shifting eyes betray her calmness.

Mother clasped her hands tightly and rested them on her desk. She stared intently at her student with piercing eyes. Krystyna tries not to blink or turn away. Finally, Mother breaks the silence. "Please sit, you appear rather tense. I hope your father is well. Are you here to ask for an envelope and stamp? Mother untangles her fingers, relaxes her face and shoulders, and pushes back in her chair. "Oh, now I remember. Your tuition check was from Aunt Jadwiga. But your father must sign the new permission form."

"Of course, Mother. Sorry to take your time."

"Kristina, you have been here five years. Yet this is the first time, if my memory serves me, that we have met like this. I know that something troubles

28

you. Not a ripple in a pond but a boulder that causes a splash. All things work for good if you love God. Help is here if you ask for it. We will never put you out or turn against you."

"That is reassuring Mother." Holding back a flood of tears, she seeks relief. "Mother, the Angelus bells. Don't you hear them?"

"Really? My hearing is not what it once was. *The angel of the Lord declared onto Mary, and she conceived of the Holy Spirit.* Time for prayer and a little lunch. Praise the Lord, it is good for the soul. I must talk to the girls about privacy for the nuns. Living in these cramped quarters will be a challenge for us all. I'm thinking out loud now. You girls are not required to pray with us. A merit system will determine who may walk to town as time and circumstances permit. You are free to go."

"Thank you, Mother. We'll make things work, I'm sure."

29

Later that day Krystyna describes her plan to Janina. "Tell Mother you'd be happy to take the mail to the post office. We must intercept the permission slip before she mails it. Oh, if she asks for me, tell her I have a bellyache. Beg her for paper and an envelope to write your family."

The scheme is successful. Krystyna forges her father's signature. Later she hides the form in the middle of a pile of papers on Mother's desk. The venue for the new school, she reads, is near the Riga River, Imperial Russia.

Chapter 5

May 1916 Riga, Russia

Bright-colored flowers turn to the sun as Mother Faustina opens her classroom windows, letting in the scented spring breeze. Her fourth-year students line up orderly according to size. At the end of the queue, a brunette with thin braided pigtails and a pale complexion enters the room followed by the girl with reddish-brown hair. Mother Superior reads from Genesis, "God asked, 'Who told you that you were naked?'"

Krystyna pulls on the ponytail hanging like a rope in front of her. "How many times have we heard this story?" she whispers.

Janina bends her arm behind herself and extends four fingers.

Leaning forward, Krystyna continues, "I wonder if they got goosebumps as they walked in the evening breeze with the Lord?" Janina nods while muffling a giggle.

Covering her mouth and turning her head, Janina whispers, "Do you suppose he had a great body like that museum statue? David, I think?"

"You two young ladies, stand up," insists Mother Faustina, slapping a wooden ruler on her desk, then her hand. " The rest of you sit up straight. Spring Fever. Learning has no season. Explain your giggling. How dare you distract us from such a sacred story."

A red-faced Krystyna stares at the ground and stammers, "So sorry, Mother. I…I was just wondering about Adam's age. Since God created Eve from his rib, he must be much older."

" Hmm… And you, Janina, where is your mind?"

Adjusting her glasses and smiling slightly, she answers, "On original blessings, Mother. You know what you told us. Everything was perfect before sin, and now so hard life has become."

"You don't know hard young lady. I'll see you both after class."

***

That evening a cool, damp breeze rattles the third-story windows of St. Sulpice, waking Krystyna from her fragmented and fitful sleep. Her attempts to regain repose are fruitless. The rhythmic breathing of her dorm mates is punctuated by squeaky bedsprings nearby. "Janina, are you awake?" she whispers.

"I suppose I am. What is it?"

"Tonight's the night, my dear friend. I'm leaving for St. Petersburg."

"Tonight? You must be kidding."

"Look out the window, Janina. It's so bright. Weren't you paying attention in science class? It's a super blue moon."

"It also looks like rain if you ask me. But hush Krystyna, we must talk, but not here. If we are caught breaking grand silence again, we'll be kneeling in the aisle for all of morning prayer. Let's head to the stairwell. Aren't you afraid?" Janina asks.

Careful to avoid loose floorboards, the pair tiptoe past the Novice sleeping in her heavily curtained cell. Silently they enter the darkened stairwell.

"I am afraid of one thing. Snakes. Ever since, my brother played a mean prank. The three of us were camping in dad's musty old canvas army tent. I think I was ten years old. It was pitch black when I crawled into the tent. I felt something moving up my leg. I screamed and ran to the house. Konrad got a proper whipping for that stunt. After that, he would harass me with snakes. His revenge."

"How dreadful," remarked Janina. "But I wish I could talk you out of this. I do know what it's like to miss your mother. My parents were divided politically. When I was ten, my mother left for the United States. Getting along with a Bolshevik husband was not easy for her. I'm still waiting for her to send for me. Your mother has been in St. Petersburg for five years now, so our histories are similar. If you're going, do it quickly. I don't know how long the moonlight will last. Do you even know the way to town?"

"A day student told me there is a shortcut along the roaring brook. It's called the river path. She drew me a map. Write to my family and explain things as best you can, please. I don't know when I'll be able to write."

"Explain? How can I do that when this makes no sense."

"Since I was a little girl, I've dreamed of Petersburg. A land of palaces, electric lights, broad cobbled streets, electrified trams, gilded carriages, Parisian fashions, the Imperial family, and political intrigue. When rumors arrived that mother was on stage, that sealed it in my mind."

"There is a war going on and a revolution. Don't you read the paper or listen to the radio? Government-controlled industries treat their workers like slaves. How does this differ from serfdom? Have you not heard of food, fuel, and housing shortages, worsened by the influx of refugees and war casualties? Striking workers are organizing against the tyranny. Only a fraction of Petrograd's people lives in luxury. Wake up. Let me see that map. A hike through the woods in the dark. Do you even know how far it is? Three miles, five miles, seven miles or more?"

"Well, if that's how you feel, forget the letter."

"Look Krystyna, you are not the only one making plans. Mother Faustina has offered me a job when I graduate next month. She wants me to teach the lower grades history, social studies, and current events."

"Does she know that your father is a personal friend of Vladimir Lenin?"

"Indeed, she does. She thinks I know more about politics than anyone else. She sees a revolution coming and she wants the girls to be educated and prepared to make good choices. You must promise me one thing Krystyna, that you will keep in touch when you reach Petrograd. My father is pressuring me to join the Bolshevik Party. He keeps me up to date about the political climate. I wish to warn you if you are in danger in the capital."

"I promise to do that." The girls turn from each other to hide tearful eyes. Krystyna continues. "You'll find my traveling bag behind the statue of

Mother Mary. Drop it out the window, please."

The pair break a long, solid, and silent embrace. Krystyna crouches behind a blooming lilac bush, taking in the fresh smells of spring. Suddenly she sees her satchel flying over her head, landing in a pile of weeds outside the convent wall. She raises her eyes to the third story. Girls are waving from every window. But no Janina. A wet-eyed Krystyna exits the convent gate, returning a weak wave to dark silhouettes pressed against the windowpanes above.

***

Charging down the stairs and into the chapel, Sister Angela finds her superior deep in prayer. "Mother Faustina, Krystyna is missing. The girls believe she's headed to the train station."

"Lord Jesus, dear sister, we've got to find her. What could she be thinking? Fetch the lorry while I go for a lantern.

And tell the Novice Mistress she's in charge til we get back."

"Right away, Reverend Mother… but we'll be breaking cloister, and it's against Russian law to leave the convent in our holy habits."

"We do not live for ourselves, dear Sister. Besides, who knows how long Russians will be in charge here. Now go!"

***

A light rain muddies the dirt road leading away from the convent and into the unknown. Krystyna takes off in a panicked run as the lorry gains ground on her. Eyeing a footpath, she abandons the road for a cornfield.

"Krystyna, stop, please!" shouted Mother Faustina as the lorry lurched to a stop. "I want to talk to you. I won't bind you or drag you back to school. I fear for your safety during these dangerous times. Plus, the rain has started. Do you want to go on?

"I do. You can't stop me."

"Of course not. But you don't even have a lantern. Do you even know the way?"

"I may be more resourceful than you think, Reverend Mother."

"And more persistent. But why? Do you think we're pressuring you to become a nun or something?" Mother asks. "Here, take this lantern."

Suddenly, Krystyna's face turns crimson, and she muffles a giggle with her hands.

"Was that such an outlandish question, my child?"

"No, Reverend Mother, it's your cap and veil. Your wings are drooping! So sorry for laughing."

"Dear Jesus, never in my fifty years as a nun have I been so embarrassed! Ow, diluted starch, in my eyes and my mouth. Don't you dare tell others of this?"

"Not a word Mother. Here's a dry babushka."

She wipes away a sticky white paste and regains her composure. "Thank you, my dear, but now back to the question."

"Although I considered it, I see a different future for myself. I'm going to Petersburg to find my mother, who I haven't seen in six years. My father told me to forget about her, to pretend she doesn't exist, but I can't do that."

"You know Krystyna, I am responsible for you. Each of my students is precious to me. Please come back with me. You will soon be of age to decide your future, but I cannot condone your actions. My rapid heartbeat is causing my whole body to shake."

"Oh, Mother, your skin is warm and clammy, and your face is red. Rest here on this rock. I will walk you back to the lorry. But I won't change my mind."

"Thank you; I will not waste more words. I entrust you to the Good Shepherd instead. I'm feeling better. Let's walk."

"Mother, you are amazing. Your color is improving. Here take my arm and watch your step. I must tell you how deeply I admire your devotion and determination during the recent crisis. How in the world did you persuade the Germans to assist you with the move?"

"Guilt my dear. It's not such a terrible word. All humanity is moral. An original blessing. You are a blessing, Be safe. Please pray for me."

"I will," promises Krystyna. "And please take special care of my friend Janina."

"Of course, but you are the one who must take care," says Mother Faustina as the two embrace. "I wish I could stop you. All of us will pray for your safe return. Yesterday I was signing diplomas. Come back for yours."

"I will. And thank you, Mother. I do love you."

"Don't make an old woman cry. Remember, you are one of only a few who have seen my thinning gray hair. Here, take this, she says, as she removes the large crucifix from her neck. For protection. I have another from a nun who left us."

"I will if God wills it. I'll remember you daily."

"You'd better. And take this lantern. I'm guessing you can use it."

Tears mix with the steady rain as the pair part ways.

Chapter 6

As the rain subsides, moonlight helps her navigate a slippery path towards the Bay of Riga. Soon cultivated land gives way to a forest of trees. Raising her kerosene lantern, sixteen-year-old Krystyna Karecki enters the dark abyss. The path descends towards a roaring river. She trips over a tree root that throws her to the ground. Two pairs of glassy eyes reflect the ambient light. Krystyna wipes muddied hands and knees on her skirt while an owl hoots above. "*What a foolish virgin I am. No oil and no oil lamp. Bless you, Mother.*" Fear dissipates into a light-hearted spirit at the next sound. *"Meow."*

Stray felines. I am not alone. Fluffy and Muffy, will you be my imaginary friends? Tell me to be brave and strong. No slimy slithering creatures Stray felines. I am not alone. Fluffy, please. Krystyna shivers at the sound of howling wolves. She descends carefully along the twisting path, keeping upright despite the roots that grab her toes. Suddenly something solid; boards under her feet. *Rest here. Stir the water. Wash your feet. Soak in the pale light. Breath in the rotting timber; the black dampness of life-giving earth.* Fatigue envelopes every aspect of her body as she collapses in a prone position. Dark clouds cancel the moonlight, and a gust of wind extinguishes her lantern. *"How foolish, no matches. Sleep. Wait for daybreak."*

The path grows steep and rocky. Krystyna climbs from the wooded darkness unto a grassy plain pierced by a meandering river. A fireball slowly rises over the shimmering water, *blinding light, so intense it hurts. Unavoidable light. How can I escape your presence? Turn and walk backwards? Cauldron of burning light, shimmering light, how will I reflect you?*

Seagulls above display their skills, landing close by to collect their applause. *"You are on the right path,"* says the voice in her head. Her jaw tightens, and her heart races as she weaves through coils of barbed wire that block her path. The acrid smell of urine mixed with feces alerts her to civilization nearby. She smells smoke, sees fire, and hears rancorous curses echoing off the water.

"Halt! Who goes there?" A young Russian soldier steps from behind a giant oak—his rifle aimed at her heart. Krystyna raises her hands, showing a snuffed lantern and her bulging wooden-handled crocheted bag. The lump in her throat hampers her speaking attempts.

"What the f--- are you doing here? Trying to get yourself killed?"

"Please, Ensign, I'm going to the train station."

"Where is your passport? What is your business?"

"I have no papers, but see here, my billet to St. Petersburg. I am a student traveling to see my mother."

"You are under arrest for trespassing on a military camp. I'll take that lantern and your bag."

"I saw no sign. Sir, take my lantern, but the bag has only clothes and personal items. Look for yourself. The rain has dampened everything."

"I'll check that bag. Empty it for me, one item at a time. Three pairs of silk hose and underwear. I'll have that velvet skirt." Krystyna hides it behind her back. The Ensign, eye to eye with her now, reaches behind her for the hemmed garment. She clutches it firmly and pulls away, but he gives it a mighty tug. *Screech!* __the sound of fingernails digging into a blackboard. The hem gives way, propelling rubles across the muddy field. Jewelry is swallowed up as well.

"So sorry sir. How stupid of me. I've never been robbed before. I'll find everything."

He grabs her arm and forces her to the ground. "You will, even if it takes an hour. Any tricks and you'll regret it."

"You're hurting me. I'll find the coins and jewelry. Twenty-five rubles, grandmother's diamond earrings, and an emerald necklace from my aunt." Her fingers, like a sieve, sift through the muck until she finds everything.

"I'll take those and the ring on your finger, your paper money, and your train ticket. You may keep the crucifix.

"You'll leave me destitute?"

"Do you prefer a bullet? Only spies sew objects in their clothes. What are you doing here?"

"Not so. I already told you, Ensign. I hid the money and jewels for security reasons. I'm not skilled at double stitching."

"Apparently not. Prove you are not a spy."

Boiling blood rises to her face, and a tightening tourniquet presses on her chest. "I see you have no heart, but you are brave, nonetheless. Your accent, your blue eyes, and your blond hair suggest Polish heritage. Am I right?"

"I am from Vilnius, conscripted two years ago." He wipes his hands on her bag and tosses it to her. "Your behavior is outrageous and dangerous. I doubt you pose a threat, but I must warn you, spies are sent to Siberia or worse. Anywhere is safer than here."

"What do you mean?"

"The war is going badly for Russia. Soldiers are losing their will to fight, even murdering their officers. Here there is talk of mutiny and desertion. When Germany attacked our harbor, we turned them back with artillery fire, but now they are preparing for a land invasion. Enough talk. Start walking."

A hundred paces later, the soldier yells, "Halt."

Krystyna turns to see her captor pulling sticks from his disintegrating boots.

"Boots come from Germany or used to. Now we get them from their dead soldiers. Not all our men have rifles. Now our bullets and our bread are rationed. We just fill the trenches with warm bodies. Our snipers do the shooting. We call it ditch warfare."

"Killing and dying. How dreadful. What is war good for? Can I dress your bleeding feet?"

"It's nothing. Move on."

Chapter 7

The path leads to a noisy group roasting rabbits for breakfast. A burly figure emerges from the shadows. "What do we have here, Comrade? A gypsy here to entice some war-weary soldiers?"

"I think not, Sergeant Rostov. She appears to be a foolhardy schoolgirl headed for the train station. I'm taking her to the Captain."

"Not so fast. My comrades and I need entertainment. We have vodka. This whore will sing and dance for us."

A pair of drunken soldiers rip Krystyna away from the young Ensign and taunt her mercilessly, pulling her head back by her braid while pouring vodka down her throat. "Sing, you harlot. You Polish swine." Krystyna collapses, sobbing hysterically. "Get up, you papist dog," taunts the drunken soldier, kicking her in the ribs and pulling her to her feet. The knife flashed in front of her face, moving to her throat. "You think we joke? Sing, or we cut off your hair or carve away those dimples".

"Give her a moment to compose herself," pleads the young Ensign.

Moments later, Krystyna wipes the tears and terror from her face. Her voice trembles. "*Ochi Chernye,* a simple folk song my father taught me." Someone strums a balalaika. Slowly and rhythmically, she moves around the campfire, singing this eerie melody:

Dark eyes burning eyes
Dark eyes flaming eyes
Always haunting me with your mystery
how I love you so
you belong to me
for eternity we shall know

Oh, these gorgeous, dark, glorious eyes
Burn with passion eyes, how they hypnotize

How I adore you so, how I fear you though
Since I saw you glow, now I love you so.

" More. Faster. Louder," the weary soldier's demand. Someone picks up the beat on an empty kettle.

Fatigue morphs into exhaustion. Krystyna collapses again, insisting, "That's all I know."

"Bitch, you could make up more words" The burly drunk grabs her from behind in a chokehold, dragging her towards an oak tree. Krystyna grabs her bag and swings it at him, catching the side of his face. "You whore. You'll pay for this."

A knife flashed in her face, rendering her immobile and panic-struck. From behind, an arm wraps around her long, slim waist and grips her tight. She feels her assailant's manhood. She digs in her heels as she's dragged across the grass. Bracing himself against a tree, he pulls her closer. "Who wants to be first?" he asks. Men slowly approach. Suddenly, Krystyna raises one knee as high as possible and plants her ankle boot into his barefoot with a mighty downward thrust. The drunk lets out a painful scream, "Bitch! You'll die for this." The grip only tightens, and Krystyna begins to slump. Suddenly Mother Faustina's words arrive," Don't step on the devil's tail; you'll lose." The bag. Searching fingers find the crucifix. Grasping it with both hands, she thrusts it over her head with all her might, landing it squarely at the bridge of his nose. "Bitch", yells the evil one as he wipes blood from his face. Krystyna slumps to the ground.

" *Crack,*" a gunshot sends chunks of dirt flying. "The next shot will give you a third eye," warns the Captain as he dismounts.

"On your knees, all of you. Hands behind your back," orders the Captain.

"Ensign, collect their weapons. You are all under arrest for mutiny and treason."

***

Later that day Captain Sergei Stepanovich Chukovsky begins an interrogation of Krystyna Karecki. "Ensign Gorski tells me you are a Polish student from the Catholic boarding school. You are traveling to the St. Petersburg, or Petrograd as it is now known."

"Yes sir, but I had no idea of the military buildup. The last time I was here, this was a beautiful public park on the bay."

"You, naïve schoolgirl, are in for many more surprises. Despite your brave, quick, and cunning action against your attacker, you are in grave danger."

"I did it to survive, nothing more. But it was you who saved me."

"Maybe so, but you humiliated an officer who now faces a firing squad. A plot may be brewing against you. I know these men."

"Then I will go to Petrograd to find my mother."

"Things are worse there. There are scandalous rumors about the Tsar, his German wife, and that peasant "monk" they are intimate with. Your only trip will be to Siberia as a political prisoner."

Krystyna stands to leave, but exhaustion overtakes her, forcing her back down. "You have no right to detain me."

"Of course, I do. But there is one way out for you."

"Tell me, for God's sake."

"I have been relieved of my post here. Reinforcements are on their way. I'm commissioned to bring wounded soldiers to Moscow. I need a nurse for the critically wounded. Your tour of duty would be six months with eight weeks of training in a field hospital there. Then you will be free. Your choice; Siberia or Moscow?"

"I will do what I must to survive."

"Good. Ensign Gorski, get her a sister of mercy uniform, one that hides her face and hair. The train leaves at dusk."

"Captain, she would appreciate a bath."

"Conceal her with this blanket Ensign, then take her to my private quarters. Others must not know of the plan."

Ensign Gorski takes Krystyna to a school building, which now serves as a barracks and munitions depot. Captain's quarters occupy part of the kitchen. Krystyna asks the Ensign, whose name she finally learns, for privacy while she lathers with lye soap and rinses off with bucket of cold water. "Tomasz, please cut off my French braid. Less breeding ground for lice."

"I need a haircut as well," says Tomasz. "And a bath."

"We better hurry. No telling when the Captain will return."

"Captain told me to help myself to a clean uniform and a new pair of boots. And I'm being promoted to a medic. So, I will accompany you to Moscow."

As the pair scramble to clean the sink and mop the floor, the door bursts open. "Who told you to cut hair?" There is rage in the Captain's eyes. A cutting look breaks across his icy face. He grabs a dirty mop and swings it at the Ensign, catching him on the side of the head. The Ensign loses his balance and crashes into the wall. He momentarily loses consciousness, awakening to the sensation of being lifted by something under his chin. The Captain's eyes flash at him, narrow, and cutting. Face to face now, he smells the Captain's dirty teeth.

"I'm sorry Sir," he cries. But the Captain keeps him pinned against the wall with a broom handle pressed to his throat.

" You must think my kindness betrays a weakness," he barks, putting all his weight into the broom handle.

"Stop. He can't breathe," pleads Krystyna.

The Captain pushes upward, lifting the boy off his feet. Krystyna grabs a potato and hurls it with all her might, missing her target. Frantically she searches the kitchen drawer and grabs a butcher knife and a rolling pin. She whacks the back of his knees, and he buckles. "Stop Captain, I have a knife and I'll use it", she demands. Tomasz wedges him away with a knee to his groin. He drops the broom and draws his revolver in a flash.

"Enough, both of you. Disrespect me again and you'll hang naked from a tree. Clean up every detail of this mess and meet me at the train station." A wry smile crosses his lips. He turns on his heels and slams the door on the way out.

"What do you suppose got into him?" Krystyna asks.

"He's deranged, I'd say."

" That's an understatement. This does not look good. Six months in Moscow with that lunatic."

"We must act like strangers in front of him. I think he is infatuated with you. Maybe you remind him of someone in the past. He approaches her, squares her shoulder parallel with his, and gazes deeply into her soft brown eyes. "I am more than fond of you. I've never met someone like you. When it's safe, I will return your valuables. I will protect you with my life."

She tilts his chin to inspect his injury. "I can treat that abrasion." Tomasz shakes his head. She moves her hand to the nape of his neck and kisses his full lips with an open mouth. "We will see, Tomasz. We will see."

Tomasz shoulders his bayoneted rifle and hands Krystyna a lantern, "Here, take this. I will distract the guards. Walk swiftly to the train station with your eyes cast down. Keep the light away from your face. Put your satchel in my duffel bag. I have you covered."

The train station is only a few city-blocks away. She mingles with commuters till she reaches the crowded platform. She paces about searching for the Captain. Moans and curses shake her core as she peers into every boxcar. "Excuse me Sister," voices a teenage soldier as he clears the way for his partner pushing a wooden wheel barrel. He unlatches the boxcar door. In the flickering light Krystyna views scores of soldiers" writhing helplessly on shelves built into the walls. On the cots in the middle of the floor, are men missing limbs. The acrid smell of decaying flesh, mixed with burnt tobacco and unwashed bodies, fills the cabin, causing Krystyna to gasp. The two soldiers find a reeking body, wrap it in a badly soiled white sheet, and dead lift it into the wheel barrel. "To the ditch comrades. Only officers receive a burial," orders the Captain. "You are looking pale and clammy, Krystyna. Your job is to change bandages and deliver shots of Vodka on the hour to those suffering from gangrene. Can you do this?"

"I can, Captain. And I will," she answers. "But where are the sleeping quarters? It has been a long day, and my soul needs rest."

"You'll sleep with your patients on the floor. We'll be in Moscow in two or three days." Tomasz waits for the Captain to leave before boarding the train and taking his place beside her.

Chapter 8

Exhausted and troubled by raw emotions, Krystyna drifts in and out of sleep on the first night of her 400-mile journey to Moscow. Her thoughts and imagination carry her back five years when she turned eleven and her father forgot her birthday. Her memories were flooded with emotional detail and vivid memories burned into her brain:

"*Tata*, is it okay for us to go down to the river?" she asks on that clean and crisp spring morning she remembers so clearly.

"Aren't you supposed to knock when you see a closed door?" answers Czeslaw, burying his face in a pillow.

"I did *Tata*, but that was a while ago. I waited for you to turn over and stop snoring."

"In ages past you would jump on the bed to wake me. So, it depends. What's the weather?"

"The rain stopped and it's sunny."

"Go ahead. But no swimming. The current is too swift."

"I bow to you father. We will be back for afternoon chores."

Eleven-year-old Krystyna skips down the stairs and meets up with her brothers who are already on the path, coasting down the hill on their bikes. "Wait for me you goons," she yells as she pedals hard to catch up. "No swimming. It's too cold anyways."

Before long the path disappears amongst the cattails and milk weeds and the mud catches bike tires, throwing the trio to damp earth. Bullfrogs croak as if talking about something important. "Wait, I lost my shoe," announces Krystyna as she plods through the mud.

"Let's keep going. We're almost to the river," suggests Konrad.

"Maybe we can build a fire and fry some fish," adds Igor. "I think we should talk about our plans for the summer."

Krystyna chimes in, "Can't remember when we talked last. You boys are off to school so often I feel like I hardly know you. Plus, I have some very important news for you."

There is a clearing and a sandy spot at the river and the siblings settle down for some breakfast. "What's the news Krystyna?" Igor asks. "Are you telling us you are getting baptized?"

"No, don't you remember. Father won't allow it. He made a promise."

"What then?"

"I got a letter from Mama. The news is she is moving to St. Petersburg. In fact, she's already there. She has a chance to become an actress."

"No way," yells Konrad. "She's not pretty enough."

"I wonder if we'll ever see her again?" asks Igor, kicking a log into the fire, knocking over the frying pan.

Suddenly Konrad jumps up and points across the river, "Look, up there on the ridge. I think it is a bison. What a rare treat. Can we get a closer view?"

"Tata said there were some around here lately, but not on our property," remarked Igor. Let's investigate further. There may be a whole herd up there."

"How can we do that?" asks Krystyna.

"The rowboat," answers Konrad. "But we'll have to bail it out first."

"The current looks swift. Can we make it?" asks Krystyna.

"You take the right oar, I'll man the left," suggests Konrad.

Igor is already in the boat, scooping out the water. With a great "heave-ho" the trio launch the boat. It doesn't take long for them to realize that nature has the upper hand in this battle. The current carries them downstream and a whirlpool tosses them into a pile of sunken timber. "We're stuck really good," laments Igor. "Now what do we do?"

"We must get out, onto the limb and see if that dislodges the boat. I've got the rope. I'll hold us steady while you get out on the log. Hold tight to the branch," instructs Konrad.

"I have a bad feeling about this," interjects Krystyna. "But it's worth a try."

"Okay, let's bounce on this log," says Igor.

The boat rises and spins, yanking Konrad into the water. He swims against the current to a clump of branches and watches helplessly as the boat disappears around a bend. "Stay where you are while I think of something," he says. "Don't panic."

Suddenly a rider on a gleaming black stallion appears on the shore. "I've been watching this farce for a while now. When I toss you the rope, loop it around your waist and hang on tight.

The rope misses its mark. Krystyna reaches for it, slipping off the slimy log. The shock of frigid water throws her into survival mode. All she feels is her fluttering heartbeat. Her toes hit the mirky, mucky bottom. Pushing off, she breaks the surface. The current slams her against a rock. Her foot is caught in a groove. She twists to free herself, gulping air and spitting out green weeds. Her eyes widen as she spies the rope snagged amongst the branches. She springs for it. *That wasn't so bad,* she tells her false self, as she is pulled to shore.

The exhausted children collapse on terra firma, laughing nervously about their misadventure. "I don't see the wisent. Maybe you were imagining things," she says to her brothers. "What are we going to tell *Tata*."

"Nothing! You hear me," shouts Konrad. "We sneak back into the mansion, change our clothes and act like nothing happened."

"Yes, one for all and all for one," Igor quips with a giggle, as the children push their mud-laden bikes up the hill.

Krystyna falls behind, favoring her sore ankle. Anatoly notices her distress, ties Midnight to a popular tree and pushes her bike. "Jump on my back if you want," he says, stooping down in an inviting position.

"Take your shirt off first," she suggests. "Give it to me. Maybe our laundry can restore the color, and its sweetness."

She wraps arms and legs around him and buries her face in curly black hair. Smells of sweaty horsehair and unwashed rider invade her senses. She sways back and forth with every step, digging her toes into his rock-hard abdominals. She closes her eyes against the blinding sun, shakes her hair in the drying breeze. *Darn, the odor is spoiling a perfect moment,* she thinks.

"Not a word of this Anatoly," cautions Konrad, "or we'll eat you for dinner."

"You are a bad actor," remarks Igor. "Thank you, Anatoly, for rescuing us. But, what about the boat?"

"I am always at your service. I will retrieve it from Lake Nitka this afternoon."

To her brothers, Krystyna remarks, "I hope someday we can regard him as an equal." Undetected by their father, they silently enter the mansion through the servant's quarters.

Chapter 9

Karecki Family Estate, Imperial Russia, May 1916

The bright horizontal sunlight penetrates the velvet drapes swaying softly in the morning breeze. Wiping sleep from his eyes, the Lord of the Manor parts the heavy drapes and greets the fresh smells of another spring morning.

"Good morning, my lord," calls Anatoly, the stable boy from below. "More refugees are muddying our fields and crossing our flooded pastures. They are begging for food and water."

"Show them to the well and the barn. But wait a minute. I will handle this situation." He grumbles and groans as he moves stiffly across the spacious bedroom to "her" closet, empty now except for a few dresses and his firearms. Returning to the open window, he loads his rifle and raises it to his shoulder. "Bam! You won't bother my cabbage again", he murmurs triumphantly.

"Anatoly, have a few peasants dress that doe. The better cuts go in the smokehouse. The rest to the barn."

"Right away, sir." Anatoly throws a leg over his cavalry horse and charges through the apple orchard in search of a butcher.

It's mid-morning when Czeslaw slowly descends the grand staircase wrapped in a Japanese silk bathrobe and knee-high black leather boots. Stuffed in his waistband is a pearl-handled Browning 45 caliber semi-auto revolver. "Irina," he calls, "spring cleaning must begin today. The children may be returning from school next week; everything must be ready." He points to the ornate Faberge table clock in the foyer. "The brass needs polishing."

"Of course, Pan Karecki. Their rooms are ready, as well as their beds."

As Czeslaw enters the barn, a dozen smartly dressed soldiers jump to their feet and fall in line. "I see you are Latvian riflemen, no doubt on your way to Riga. But what of these refugees?"

"On their way to the heartland," answers a senior officer. "They have been marching for hundreds of miles."

" You are welcome to stay and rest, but my spies tell me the Germans are encamped only miles from here. Enjoy the venison and fight bravely in Riga."

Barking dogs draw his attention outside. Drawing his revolver, he aims at the snarling wild boar held at bay by a half-dozen wolfhounds. One shot silences the boar and the dogs. "*Stara baba,* this carcass is for you and your family," he yells, calling the old peasant from her cook fire.

"More meat for my children. Thank you, master. Please come to our barbecue. Your visitors are invited as well."

To the refugees and soldiers, he says, "You poor souls, stay as long as you want. The bridge is washed out, and we have only one rowboat. However, my woodsmen have constructed a high wire platform to get folks and their gear over the stream quicker. The tanners have designed harnesses to carry people. I've used it, so it's safe for anyone under three hundred pounds. The opposite bank is twenty feet higher, so our strongest loggers must work harder to pull the load across using pulleys and cogwheels. The children around here have the best time, getting a free ride over and zipping back at great speed. Come, I will show you". Herons and ospreys take flight as Czeslaw's sinking steps follow the deep muddy path to the submerged dock. "The current is swift, but my loggers can get you across. Their strength is incredible. Try your luck at fishing if you like but make your own poles. Ours were stolen, like so much else around here. Speaking of which, I had to build a cage around the tower and lock it at night, to prevent the teenagers from using the zip line. It made me angry that kids see kindness as weakness and try to take advantage. But with their parents off to the Tsar's war, they lack supervision. If the peasants side with the revolutionary forces, it will be the end of Russia as we know it. The socialists and the Bolsheviks promise a better tomorrow, but I have my doubts. Hard choices are ahead for all of us."

The senior officer bows profoundly, "On behalf of all of us, we are most grateful for your gracious hospitality."

"You Lieutenant and your men are welcome to camp up by the house, away from the farm animals."

"Most gracious of you, my lord. I am Lieutenant Ryszard Brzezinski of Riga."

"I bow to you sir. I am Pan Czeslaw Karecki, lord of this manor. It is an honor to meet a Polish nobleman from another district. Come see my home and enjoy our hospitality."

"It will be an honor, sir. Your name is known by my countrymen for your work with refugees."

Czeslaw spends a good part of the afternoon touring the grounds and explaining to his new friend the changing fortunes of the manor since the abolition of serfdom in 1861. Together they climb the u-shaped staircase to the main portico and enter the parlor and grand ballroom. The far wall is dominated by a masonry fireplace, stove, and chimney reaching high into the vaulted ceiling. Two crossed lances, eighteen feet in length and draped with the war banners of the Polish winged knights, are mounted there. Above the mantle hangs a hand-carved replica of the family crest from the Commonwealth era, awarded to the estate by the office of Polish Heraldry. Life-size portraits of King Zymunt III (1566-1632) and Stanislaw Karecki (1567-1626) flank the fireplace on each side.

"Stanislaw is the grand knight of the Karecki family. He was rewarded 5,000 acres by Polish King Zymunt III for defense of Sebehz Castle against the invading Russians in 1590. The estate has been subdivided many times over the years as family members have claimed inheritance. Ryszard, I am left with only 500 acres."

Ryszard's eyes are transfixed on the banners and lances above the fireplace. He reaches into a breast pocket for his bifocals and examines the relics. "Real?" he asks.

"Henryk Sienkiewicz, of *Quo Vadis* fame, asked the same question when he visited in 1880," answered Czeslaw. "He thought the lances were actual war replicas from the Riga battle of 1605, when in truth only the steel spear points are relics. Our woodcarver fashioned the lances in our workshop, hollowing out the middle according to specifications so they are practically authentic," explains Czeslaw.

They pass through the dining hall with its huge mahogany table surrounded by dozens of matching chairs. The table is set for four. "Roast duck at six, Ryszard. But let's finish the tour and enjoy some refreshments." They crossed the hall to the sparsely furnished chapel. Beneath a sizable crucifix on the far wall is an elevated marble altar and gold-plated tabernacle, empty now. Part of the altar rail remains. Czeslaw kneels to offer a brief prayer. They pause to soak in the colors of the stained-glass window filtering through the brilliant sunlight, one depicting the baptism of Jesus in the Jordan and the other the Parable of the Prodigal Son. "Are you Catholic, Ryszard?"

"When it comes to religion, Pan, I am a believer but a fallen-away follower. But please excuse me as I must return to my troops."

"So be it," responds Czeslaw. "Duty calls I suspect".

Morning gives way to sweltering afternoon heat. Czeslaw finds Irina in the dining hall resetting the table.

"Our guest has taken his leave. His troops are on the move again. Here is his apology note. You and I alone in this house again." She curtsies and leaves Czeslaw to his thoughts.

Chapter 10

"Stop your cleaning and join me for a drink," insists Czeslaw as he directs Irina to the parlor. "Please stop calling me 'my lord'. It doesn't fit today."

" Of course. As you wish, sir. I will try but it's not always easy."

"Irina, my trusted servant, I am feeling quite melancholy today, living alone in this huge house. Without the children around, life is empty and meaningless."

"But that will change soon, Czeslaw. I miss them as well."

His eyes are fixed on the well-dated family portrait on the credenza. "Just the four of us. My heart aches, and I am bitter toward their mother for leaving. The hurt won't go away. It's been with me every day for the past six years. And now I'm realizing my part in the breakup."

"You mean besides the drinking."

"Touché, one drunk speaking to another."

"What part? Pan Karecki."

"You heard our arguments. I insisted that the children be baptized in the Catholic church. My wife and her family accuse me of treason. *How dare you defile Russian law and disrespect the Tsar*, they would say. *Make the sign of the cross the Russian way, right to left with three fingers.* "Was it all really worth all the fighting?"

"Maybe you were just trying to please your father. His death when you were but sixteen left you responsible for this estate and the Karecki legacy spanning how many generations?" Irina asked.

"Eight. My father our last Polish noble due to the new laws. Russification, how I hate that word."

"Let us raise another glass of vodka to him." The pair rocked back in their chairs. "I promised him a male heir. Proud to give him two. But deny my ethnicity and my Catholic faith? No chance. Call it Congress of Poland, or Duchy of Poland, or Russian Poland, it doesn't matter. *Poland will always be Poland if the Vistula flows free.* Something to drink for, don't you think?

"We have this bottle of vodka to finish. *Na zdrowie* Czeslaw. My least favorite word is serfdom. I was fourteen when it was abolished. I'm grateful your father gave us a piece of land, and you gave me a job."

"I'll drink to that as well. *Na zdrowie.*"

A few days later

"Hurry, Anatoly," Irina yells to the stableboy as she hurries down the stone steps of the white-washed manor. "Hitch up Midnight. You've got to fetch the Doctor quickly, or the Pan may die.

He's having those chest pains again, and he's red as a beet. Hurry."

Three hours later, Dr. Mikhail Ivanovich Trebova is gently pouring hot mint tea, laced with molasses and medicinal herbs, down the throat of his friend Pan Czeslaw Karecki. "Rest, Pan Karecki," he advises with a warm, assuring smile. "You are burning up, and your heart is racing. Here, keep these cold packs on that broad forehead of yours. And no smoking and no vodka for the next three weeks."

"That's how you treat a friend, aye?" Czeslaw murmurs in a weak voice as he nods off to sleep.

Picking up a piece of crumpled paper, he exits with Irina. "What set your Master off, do you suppose?" he asks.

"That telegram just arrived this morning. I don't know what it says".

Adjusting his glasses, Dr. Trebova reads aloud:

Dear Pan Karecki, May 11, 1916

Your daughter Krystyna absconded from our convent boarding school last night. The local authorities have been alerted.

We are surprised, distraught, and confused by this event.

Please be assured that Krystyna, to our knowledge, was not mistreated in any way. There is a rumor she is headed to Petrograd.

Sending many prayers for her safety.

Your faithful servant,
Sister Faustina of Mary
Mother Superior
St. Sulpice Convent School
Riga, Russia

Blood drains from Irina's face. "Holy Mother of God! I can't believe this. Whatever has gotten into that strong-willed child? And Riga? How did she get there?"

The Doctor wipes his brow. "I have no idea. But these are very troubling times. People are acting out of character. "And what of Igor and Konrad?" Trebova asks. "When will they return from military school?"

"They are due in Sebehz next Wednesday. Konrad will begin University studies.

Anatoly will pick them up," Irina continues. "My heart goes out to them. How would they manage if they lost their father?"

Irina nods, "All this suffering over religion, nationality and who knows what."

"And now war and more talk of revolution," adds the Doctor. "The current Tsar, God bless him, is ill-equipped to rule a county as vast as ours. And he has made so many bad decisions; first, the disastrous war with

Japan followed by the massacre of those peaceful demonstrators on Bloody Sunday.

"I need you both," comes a weak voice from the bedroom. "I lost control of Krystyna. The Sisters have done a commendable job. But now she has run away. I must find her. What could she be thinking? She must think herself old enough to make her own decisions, including the Catholic question. I will find her."

"Czeslaw, you have just suffered a mild heart attack. You cannot travel, especially if you have no idea where she is", offered Trebova. "You want your children to be Catholic. But Why?"

" My friend, I hardly have the energy to begin. But look in the safe," pointing to the black box under his desk. Fetch the key from the window ledge."

Lifting the heavy lid Trebova carefully removes some fragile artifacts one by one until he comes upon a leather-bound document. Holding in up to the light he read the Russian title aloud, <u>My Polish Heritage</u> by Jadwiga Karecki. "Yes, my sister's creative essay from high school. Written some fifty years ago. Read it aloud so we all can appreciate it."

"Of course, Pan Karecki. Are you able to stay awake?"

"Yes, without a doubt.

Chapter 11

My Polish Heritage- by Jadwiga Karecki, May 1885

Preface

My dear teacher and fellow students, inspiration to write this essay comes from a memorable encounter with famed Polish author Henryk Sienkiewicz, whose works include <u>With Fire and Sword: An Historical Novel of Poland, Sweden, and Russia </u>(1884). In March of this year, a postal letter addressed to our late father Alexander arrived. My brother Czeslaw opened it and was astonished by its content. Henryk explained that through contact with the Office of Polish Nobility, *he learned of several Karecki knights who died in the war to save Old Poland from the invading Swedes. He requested verification. We met him in a Riga tavern and were able to provide documentation, proving two Kareckis, Jan and Samuel, lead a spirited charge against the Swedish hordes in 1660. The battle was near the Polish village of Golamb on the Vistula River. These great-grandsons of Stanislaw lead the charge, but we're later cut down by canon fire. Sienkiewicz included this historical detail in his epic novel, <u>Deluge</u> (Volume II, Chapter 27). With this background I can begin my story.*

1605-Krakow, Poland

Grand Knight Stanislaw Karecki and King Zygmunt III of

Poland were relishing a mug of mead in the King's royal palace while discussing important political and religious matters which would affect the future of central and Western Europe for centuries to come. The two friends were political allies for over 20 years, dating back to the day Stanislaw gave a rousing speech on the parliamentary floor endorsing him to become the next King of Poland. Stanislaw was a well-educated Polish landowner. He was a Polish feudal Lord who moved the family, the peasants, and serfs to this remote part of the Kingdom which was once Lithuania before the meager with Poland. Here as a grand knight, he could help secure the Commonwealth's border with Russia. Stanislaw earned his nobility and the manorial estate, which included Lake Nitka and the peasant hamlet of Glembochino. He built a huge horse farm where he could train the finest stallions for the Polish cavalry, known also as the Winged Hussars. Polish horsemen adopted light laminated armor and open helmets. Their aim was to frighten their enemy by a full, lighting charge. The sight of wings (wooden slats with attached eagle, falcon, or vulture feathers) fastened to wooden harnesses would panic enemy horsemen and pikemen just by the sound. Their lances were extra-long, up to eighteen feet, and light weight because they were hollow. A speeding wall of impaling lances and trampling horses horrified many a foe. After the charge, the hussars would turn quickly to finish off the enemy with saber and muskets.

Ambitious King Zygmunt petitioned the Polish parliament (Sejm) to carry out a siege in Moscow which was successful. The

91

Polish-Lithuanian Commonwealth was at the height of its power and influence. This was indeed the golden age of Poland. But in two brief centuries this vast country, formed by the annexation of Lithuania would be wiped off the map of Europe.

The two friends were talking about religion. Zygmunt's vision was to become the King of Sweden as well as Poland/Lithuanian with hopes to turn back the tide of Protestantism. He also wanted to spread Catholicism throughout neighboring Orthodox Russia.

The King elicited a profession of faith from his knight. "Do you believe in the Mass, Stanislaw, where the sacrifice of Christ as the lamb of God is made present again to take away the sins of the world?"

"Yes Sir, of course I believe."

"And Stanislaw, do you believe Christ, true God and true man, is present under the appearance of bread and wine when it is consecrated by the priest?"

" Yes Sir, of course I believe."

"Then what can we do together to spread the Kingdom of God throughout Poland?"

" I would like you to send a highly educated Jesuit priest to my estate and the hamlet of Glembochino. We need the sacraments, and our peasants need education in the Catholic faith."

"And what, Stanislaw, will you do for me?"

" I will give 100 of my finest steeds to strengthen your famous cavalry."

"The deal is struck, Stanislaw. I will visit your estate in the year of our Lord, 1611. Prepare your family and your peasants well."

"So be it, your Majesty."

For three years the whole village was alert in anticipation of the King's visit. Peasants and serfs, as well as the noble family were schooled in the basic beliefs of the Catholic faith thanks to a visiting priest. The Karecki family helped prepare many for baptism.

1611, Glembochino, Poland

Five-year-old Martin was startled out of his sleep by the high-pitched screams of his eight-year-old sister. "The King is coming. The King is coming", exclaims Little Danusha, reacting to the news. "When will he arrive, Mama? Will his wife and children be coming too? I'd love to have someone to play with."

"Danusha dear, he's coming with his cavalry to collect *Tata's* promise of horses. He's bringing an important guest, Fr. Jan, who will be giving you your first Communion."

"Mama, I can't wait".

" You'll be wearing the pretty white dress and veil I've been sewing for you."

" I'm so happy. And how long will the King stay?"

" Just three days Sweetie."

"Oh Mama, we have the very best life here, don't we?"

"Yes darling, something we should be thanking God for every day."

" I do Mama, but I worry for the peasants who work so hard and have so little."

"That's why we should pray every day for a better world. *Tata* is trying hard to give them a better life. With the help of Fr. Jan, *Tata* will start a school in the village so young people can learn to read and write."

"I love *Tata* so much."

" Me too, my dear Danusha, me too."

"But why does *Tata* have to go off to war with the King. I worry terribly."

"To make Poland strong so no one can take away our land, our way of life, my dearest one."

"I don't understand, *Matka*. But I will pray for God's better answer."

"You are so wise my dear. And before I forget, when you do receive Communion, do not chew the wafer. Peel it from the roof of your mouth with your tongue."

"I'll remember Mama. I don't want Jesus to suffer more because of me."

"You have a good heart, my child."

"I love you, Mama."

"Not as much as I love you, my dearest darling."

***

So, on April 4th, 1611, the villagers of Glembochino witness a cloud rising above the dusty road to their humble village. Hundreds of peasants and serfs line both sides of the road. Every woman's head is covered by a babushka. Suddenly the King's entourage stops and from the Royal carriage emerges King Zygmunt and Fr. Jan Zaleski, S.J., the newly ordained Jesuit priest. The crowd is struck completely silent. Zygmunt orders his cavalry to dismount and join festivities with the host family and their guests. On a hilltop Fr. Jan sets up a simple altar and celebrates Mass for the faithful. After Mass he places a consecrated host in an ornate golden receptacle and leads a procession through the village. Villagers fall on bent knees and cross themselves. At the center of the village Stanislaw and Zygmunt invoked a confession of belief: "I believe in my heart and openly profess that the bread and wine that are placed on the altar are, through the mystery of the sacred prayer and the words of the Redeemer, substantially changed into the true and proper and life-giving flesh and blood of Jesus Christ our Lord, and that after the consecration they are truly the body of Christ." After the singing of traditional Latin hymns and ritual prayers, the crowds is dismissed, thus ends the first day of King Zygmunt's visit.

***

The next morning Zygmunt, his wife and children rise to the sound of roosters crowing. They had been given full use of the ten-room Karecki mansion which overlooks acres of rolling hills and valleys, forest, and cultivated farmland. The

Karecki family accommodated the King and his entourage by making the manor house available to their guests. At sunrise Fr. Zaleski celebrated Mass for the host, hostess, and distinguished guests in the spacious ballroom. Danusha received her first Holy Communion. Afterwards, a sumptuous breakfast of kielbasa, eggs, biscuits, and tea was served. Hearty souls bath and swim in frigid Lake Nitka and later join a military parade and folk festival in the nearby town of Sebezh, an important Polish fortress. At sundown a lavish dinner is served at the Karecki manor.

***

The day's excitement is too much for little Martin and sister Danusha. They cannot fall asleep that evening. Instead, they sneak out of their tent and return to the house unnoticed. For the next three hours they listened to *Tata*, the King, and other nobles discuss and debate Poland's future role in international politics. Though the children understood little, they sense the dangers ahead for Poland.

"What in heaven's name are you doing out of bed!" Mama cries when she finds her missing children. After a calculated scolding she hugs and kisses them and tucks them back in bed with her.

Stanislaw renews his commitment to help Zygmunt capture Moscow for the Commonwealth. Fr. Zaleski accepts the post of chaplain for the Karecki family and moves into the log cabin erected for him. The Karecki family often pray the rosary in the newly constructed chapel inside the manor. Fr. Jan vows to build a church for the growing Catholic community of Glembochino.

***

In the morning King Zygmunt, Stanislaw, and the hussars gather 100 trained war horses and prepare for departure and the impending battle for Moscow. But first Zygmunt needed to thank the Karecki family for their hospitality. He also charmed Danusha by addressing her directly. "And what would you like to be when you grow up?"

" I'd like to be a Princess, then the Queen."

"So, maybe you would like to marry my youngest son someday. He is not much older than you."

"No, your Majesty, I don't want to marry a Prince, I want to be a Princess, then Queen of Poland, or maybe King, just like Queen Jadwiga who took the title of King of Poland in 1568."

"Well, you know your history. Keep the dream alive sweet

Danusha," the King says with a chuckle. "I wish you well."

Nobility

Martin, Stanislaw's only son, is a noble by birth. In Old Poland nobility is inherited through bloodline, not achievement. When his father dies, Martin (20) inherits the estate and voting rights in the Polish parliament (Sejm). But it is Danusha who, in 1626, showed an interest in politics. She engaged her father in an earnest discussion before he passed away.

"Tata, where do you think Poland is heading? What do you think about Zygmunt III's reign?"

"To be honest, Danusha, I believe he is good at spreading the faith, but I worry for the future of Poland."

"What do you mean, Tata?"

"I think it was a mistake to invade Russia during their "time of trouble." We only held Moscow for two years. We do not have secure borders and we are threatened by Russia, Sweden, Prussia, and Austria. How many invaders can we hold off?"

"I'm with you, Father. No more unnecessary wars."

***

In time Danusha becomes an ardent pacifist and the family's first "feminist." She is miffed at her lack of status. She is granted no opportunity for higher education, and her future husband is selected based on _his_ nobility. When her brother becomes sickly with emphysema, she devises a plot to take his place in the Sejm. She cuts off her hair, wraps bandages around her chest, learns his handwriting, dresses in his military uniform and travels to

Warsaw to become a voting member of the Sejm.

However, her work and her voting in the Sejm cannot secure peace between the Commonwealth and Sweden. Sweden invades Poland, causing massive destruction and loss of life. Two of Martin's grandsons, as lieutenants, lead a charge against the Swedes but are killed in battle (1660).

Meanwhile, Danusha discovers she is comfortable in men's garb. Corsets, silk lingerie, silk stockings, and full-hopped dresses are repugnant and impractical for her horse-breeding career. She forfeits her nobility to marry an artisan from the village. They partner to teach horsemanship skills to women of noble birth. They contract with the King of Poland/Lithuania to produce war-ready horses for his army.

Historically, ongoing wars with Muscovy (Russia), Sweden, and the Ottoman Empire weakened Greater Poland's power during the next century. Finally in 1795, Poland ceased to exist as an independent country due to political conspiracy by dominant neighboring countries. Prussia, Austria, and Russia divided the once-mighty nation. Proud, defiant, and resistive rebels declare, "Poland is not dead as long as we live." Other patriotic Poles declared, "Poland will remain Poland as long as the Vistula flows. We love that lazy river flowing through central Poland, but we lament that it runs red with the blood of our countrymen."

A Great Adaptation

Both Poland and our family had to make uncomfortable

adjustments in 1795 due to Russian imperialism. The last King of Poland/Grand Duke of Lithuania was Stanislaw II Augustus, who reigned from 1764 to 1795. No more King; ethnic Poles would need to swear fealty to the Russian Tsar. Our estate was now in Russia. Religious freedom would soon become an issue. Since we lost a market for horses, our family took up farming and husbandry. The estate would become less profitable as new taxes were imposed, first on the property, then based on the number of household members, including the peasants and serfs who labored there. The Sejm was disbanded. Religious customs were threatened by Orthodoxy, the official state religion. All legal documents required Russian script. Some of our family moved to central Poland, near Warsaw, where some self-governing was allowed in "the Duchy of Poland."

More Family Folklore

In 1860, several of the Karecki children engage in an animated discussion on Holy Scripture. Irene (20) challenges her siblings, "How can we bring good tidings to the poor?"

" What would Jesus do if He were here in Glembochino?", asks Ryszard, Irene's shy twin brother.

"He wouldn't be feeding the poor" answers Edzio (24), the twins' older brother.

" Why is that?" asks 10-year-old Thaddeus.

"Because He was poor himself. He had nothing to give away", answers Edzio.

"But what about when He multiplied the loaves and the fishes and fed 5,000?", Thaddeus asks.

"Reread the story. He had the disciples search the crowd for what could be shared. A little boy had five loaves of bread and two fish. Not much but he shared all that he had."

"Oh! I think I get it. Jesus needs us to get the job done."

"We have so many fruits and vegetables in the barn that can't be sold. Let's give them to the hungry", suggests Ryszard.

"I'm for that", says Irene. " And what else can we do? "

"Let's just use our favorite hobbies and our talents to help the peasants who do not enjoy our privileged lifestyle." offers Edzio.

"But do we dare defy *Tata* who does not want us to interact even socially with the peasants?" Irene asks.

"I think that's partially your fault." Thaddeus offers. "He's aware of how your eyes light up every time you see Boris the Blacksmith hard at work in the barn."

"What would you know about that kind of thing?"

"I know stuff," answered Thaddeus.

"I know that *Tata* would prefer that we distance ourselves from the peasants, but I sense a higher value here."

"Whatever, Edzio. But back to your other idea, I love to fish in Lake Nitka, but what can I do. I'm only ten years old."

Edzio, pausing, as if deep in thought, adds, "I've got some ideas about that. Let me research it."

Irene speaks up. "I'm pretty darn good with the needle. I'm going to start sewing dresses for the peasant girls in the village.".

"You know what?", voices Ryszard, "I'd like to see more fresh ham and kielbasa for everyone."

When Tata gets wind of his children's plans, he is furious. However, Irene convinces him that she has no romantic interest in Boris and shows him how their efforts to help the peasants would improve the family finances. Reluctantly he breaks with tradition and allows his children to work directly with the peasants.

It doesn't take long for the Karecki children to put their plans into action. With Edzio's help, Thaddeus introduced carp farming in Lake Nitka. This improves the nutrition of all the villagers because of a new "keep what you catch" policy on the lake. Irene teaches sewing to the villagers. Next, she imports fifty pedal-driven stitching machines so dresses and other clothing can be mass-produced. Ryszard introduces collective pig and poultry farming. He helps the villagers build a biogas digester which turns animal waste into methane gas and fertilizer. The gas powers a huge smokehouse for locally processed hams, sausages, and bacon. Finally, the Karecki children solve the problem of surplus apples. They convince their father to build a cider mill on the swollen creek. Thus, Glembochino becomes a popular commercial trade center in Vitebsk province, Russia.

***

The Dreaded Russification

Polish landowners led a rebellion against Russian rule in 1863. Because the fight for Polish sovereignty was unsuccessful Russia was able to impose punitive consequences. Tsar Alexander II was threatened by Polish nationalist who were well educated and politically motivated to restore Poland to nationhood. In 1864, he prohibited the use of Polish language in public places. Next, Polish could no longer be taught or used in schools. It became illegal to teach Polish or the history of Poland. Religious freedom was restricted. Orthodoxy was the official religion of Russia. Education and baptism in the Catholic faith was forbidden. Catholic Churches were demolished or re-purposed. Many Catholic priests were expelled. However, Polish resistance continued. One form of defiance was carried out by an underground network of Polish educators. They taught the Polish language and instructed children in the Catholic faith.

In Glembochino Jerome Karecki and his brother Fr. Michael Karecki, S.J., a Jesuit priest, saved their beloved parish church from destruction. Through their efforts it was converted into a Russian Orthodox Church. The new rituals would take place in a familiar venue.

***

A Changing Landscape

In 1861 Tsar Alexander II ended serfdom in Russia. "What does this mean for us?" Alexander Karecki asks his cousin Casimir. "Serfs will no longer be tied to the land nor obligated and subservient to the landowner. They will be equal to the peasants and therefore free to pursue whatever work they can find. Also, they have the right to be landowners."

" I will share my profits with the peasants and former serfs 50/50.

One bushel of apples goes to the estate, the next one goes to the worker," boasts Alexander.

"I better not comment. But at least it is a contract of employment. Something the serfs never had before," Casimir observed. "No offense, but I propose a cash settlement for my portion of the estate. I have business interests to pursue in Riga."

That, my dear readers, is my father and uncle speaking. Alexander, my father, applied to the Secretary of Polish nobility for a family tree for Stanislaw's branch of the Karecki ancestors. My brother Czeslaw acquired the Estate when my father died in 1868. The part that vexes me is that forty relatives over eight generations have been recognized as nobles, but not one female. I have lost the rich history of the strong, amazing women relatives. History has forgotten them; their birth, their death, even their names. When It comes to the Kareckis or Polish nobility, it's all about the sperm. Furthermore, it appears that most of history is written by men and about men. Women write diaries which are eventually discarded. When I am of age, I will ask Czeslaw for my half of the estate. I will pursue a socialist agenda. I know this will end my relationship with my brother, but I will live my truth.

Many other Karecki relatives take their inheritance and move to central Poland where liberal laws allow more freedom to practice religion and cultural traditions.

The End

by Jadwiga Karecki - November 15, 1885

***

Czeslaw opens heavy eyes. "Yes, Jadwiga claimed the northern half of Lake Nitka and the surrounding five hundred acres, but she is pushing a socialist agenda. She subdivided the land and gave plots to peasants for collective farming. It's a half-baked idea if you ask me."

"Drink your tea." Trebova directs. Irina props another pillow under his head and brings the steaming mug to his mustache. "Get your rest," says bleary-eyed Irina. She kisses his forehead, blows out the candles, tiptoes out of the room, and gently closes the door.

Chapter 12

Petrograd, Imperial Russia - December 18, 1916

The sun was already setting when the train from Moscow screeched into the station at 3:30 PM. A long fur coat covers her white uniform to the bottom of fur-lined boots. Krystyna joins a huge crowd of Petrograd socialites and curious commoners peering over the narrow bridge crossing the frigid Nera River. Last night police pulled the mutilated body of Grigori Rasputin from its icy tomb. Below the bridge, a group of elderly women chop ice to find frigid water. "May this water, washed in Fr. Grigori's blood, bring strength and healing to the suffering poor of Russia," prays an old peasant woman.

"May his martyrdom save Russia from revolution," prays another.

Voices from the bridge echo off the frozen river. "He was no saint! Nothing but a lecherous old fool who cast an evil hypnotic spell on the Tsar and Tsarina. Good riddance to him." Another angry voice adds, "Mark my word, the old regime will fall with him."

Krystyna joins a procession, led by two Orthodox bishops, one carrying a pectoral processional cross, the other bearing an icon to Our Lady of Kazan. Onlookers join the pilgrims moving toward the police station, intent on viewing Rasputin's remains. The rhythmic chanting of a traditional prayer quiets the crowd. "Lord Jesus Christ, son of the Living God, have mercy on us sinners." Krystyna weaves through the crowd. Her eyes search covered faces sheltering from the cold, bitter wind. She flashes a photo of her mother but the crowd denies that they know her. The procession passes the windswept facades of the Hermitage and Winter Palace, then turns up the broad cobblestone street of Nevsky Prospect.

The Chief of Police stops the crowd. "No one may see him 'til the autopsy is complete," he insists. "The conspirators must be brought to justice."

A bystander mounts a soapbox, yelling, "A hero's medal for the assassins. Let the Tsar be next."

Krystyna follows the crowd into the Kazan Cathedral asking believers if they know Tanya Karecki. Finally, someone answers, "I think she is a seamstress. Ask in the Singer Building," pointing to the six-story modern structure across the Prospect. Christmas lights and garlands add warmth to the impressive architecture built in the Art Nouveau style. The lights climb from the entrance to the glass tower capped by a majestic dome, rivaling the Cathedral's onion spires for dominance.

"Visitors must take off their boots," says the doorman as he helps

Krystyna with her bag. "We rolled up the red carpet and sent it out for cleaning. The name is unfamiliar but check out those ladies with the prayer beads. I think there may be a seamstress in their midst."

She slides across the marble floor, taking a seat near chanting women huddled around an icon. Surveying the crowd her eyes fixate on a silver broach resting on the bosom of a stately woman. Their eyes meet.

"Krystyna! Holy Lord Jesus! Is that you? Whatever are you doing in Petersburg?"

"Lord bless this day. Mama, I can't believe I found you."

Hugs and kisses turn to rhythmic sobbing. "Come child and warm up. Your teeth are still chattering," suggests Tanya, the estranged wife of Czeslaw Karecki. "We have so much to talk about. I must know, how are you and dear Konrad and Igor? There is hardly a day I don't think of you and pray for your safety and well-being."

"Please, Mother. Truly unbelievable." An unspoken thought enters Krystyna's mind as she glances away, *I hope the warmth of your home fire and a simmering cup of boiling sweet tea will thaw my cold and bitter heart.*

"My dearest child," she says, taking her by the arm and forcing a smile. Together after all these years. Come, let's ride the lift. Have you ever been on an elevator? "

Krystyna shakes her head. "This building and the Palace and all of St. Petersburg is so hauntingly beautiful. I can't wait to see it all."

"I will guide you. Come, I have a magnificent view of the venues you seek from our sixth-floor observatory."

Krystyna gazes in awe at the magnificent Baroque architecture. "The boys are well, in military school. But then again, I haven't seen them in six months. When my fingers and toes are no longer numb, I'll tell you more."

Tanya opens her tiny, windowless apartment. "I am a live-in housekeeper for foreign diplomats who live here. I can say no further. The pot-belly stove will give us warmth."

"Mother, I think you can guess why I am here. As a woman, I need to know why you left your husband and children. Father said he wanted a divorce after you left, but it's practically impossible according to Russian law."

"I dread to speak ill of your father, but I can only offer my opinion if you want to know what came between us."

"Of course, Mother, I want your side of the story."

"I found him cold and indifferent, as well as arrogant and self-absorbed. I thought him obsessed with preserving his Polish heritage and customs in defiance of Russian law. His allegiance was to the Pope. Mine was to the Tsar. And when he insisted that you children be baptized by a papist priest, that was it for me. I threatened to have him arrested."

"I remember those arguments about who was God's appointed and anointed representative here on Russian soil. I found the debate frivolous and trivial. You know, he sent us to Polish Catholic school after you left. I do appreciate the excellent education I received but more later. Please continue Mother."

"That's wonderful to hear. Truthfully, I never wanted to marry your father. He was a widower, twenty-five years older than me. Our family doctor suggested the match and my parents considered him an eligible bachelor.

"Are you referring to Dr. Trebova?"

"Yes, Czeslaw was married to his sister. Sadly, she died of cholera when they were both in their twenties. He loved her dearly. He never got over her, I'm told."

"I never knew that. Father never spoke of it. Did they have any children?"

"No, to my knowledge. I wasn't much older than you, eighteen, when we met. I found him stiff in the collar, always bragging about his Polish nobility. I remember the wedding. My stomach was in a knot, and I had to fake a smile all day long, while feeling numb and empty. But I gave him three beautiful children whom I love with all my heart. He wasn't happy either. I suggested we travel, vacation in Odessa or St. Petersburg, or to his beloved Poland. He was not the least bit interested. When he began drinking, I couldn't take it anymore."

"Did he beat you, Mama?"

"Oh no, my dear. I would have left in a heartbeat and would have taken you all with me if it ever came to that.

But you must promise me one thing. You are not to tell the boys any of this. They adore him so."

"I understand and I agree Mama. But why didn't you write?"

"But I did! Once a week for over six months," insists a teary-eyed Tanya. "Then I realized that Czeslaw would never allow you to read the letters. So, I began keeping a journal instead. Letters to my Darling Daughter."

"Mother, I believe what you say. Do you remember the family album we had? When Papa learned that you left the district for St. Petersburg to pursue a career, all the photos of you and us together vanished."

"My dear, it doesn't surprise me in the least. I'm sure he destroyed the precious icons I had to leave behind as well."

"No matter Mama," comments Krystyna. "It's all in the past. I knew I would see you again when I became of age. So, tell me everything that happened."

"Well, dearest darling, I returned to my parents after Czeslaw and I separated. I was quite depressed for over a year. I was hardly able to get out of bed. Then a cousin of mine invited me to St. Petersburg. She was an actress at the Mariinsky Theater. I worked as a seamstress for Singer Company. After two years of evening acting lessons, I auditioned with the *Nevsky Farce,* a Russian comedy club devoted to a parody of Russian high society. Keeping my seamstress job and housekeeping here pays my room and board. I'm so grateful to be in the best part of town, just blocks from where people are living in squalid conditions. I'm on the verge of tears again, Krystyna, as I think of the boys. I don't know when I'll see them again. Your father has such a hold on them. To think that Igor is already 13 and Konrad is 16. Hard to believe. I have so much more to tell you, but I need to hear everything about you and your plans."

"I've been working as a nurse in Moscow, assisting in the operating room where doctors amputate the limbs of poor boys returning from the Front. Besides sterilizing instruments and assisting the doctors, I had to give the body parts a respectful burial. It wasn't a pleasant experience, but I did it, and here I am. I want to see all the sights; the Winter Palace and Hermitage, the Conservatory of Music and Academy of Arts, the Alexandrinski and Mariinsky theaters, the Cathedral of St. Isaac, and the Bronze Horseman, of course."

"Sweet princess, I could never do what you did, but I will show you the city. It has truly been a long day. See, that carton of letters over there? They are yours, but again, not for the boys."

"Oh Mother, it must be hundreds of pages long. It will take me weeks to read."

"Perhaps so but let us rest now."

"The days are so short and oh so cold. Good night, Mother. I can hardly believe I am here with you."

"Sweet dreams, my child."

***

But dreams are hard to come by as an anxious and restless girl tosses and turns on her mother's ragged couch. Stumbling in the dark, she finds the desk and a match to light the oil lamp. Opening the leather-bound journal, she picks up a loose page lying on top. Her heart jumps to her throat, and her hands tremble as she reads.

December 15, 1916
Dear Krystyna,

The chaos on the streets of Petrograd is unbelievable. Revolutionaries are everywhere stirring the pot of discontent. I'm afraid the old order is passing away. Tsar Nicolas made himself supreme commander of the army. His failure is evident to everyone. Meanwhile, Tsarina Alexandra and Father Grigori are running the government. Some say they have an inappropriate relationship. Refugees from Poland, Latvia, Lithuania, and Jews from the ghettos are flooding the city. Support for the Tsar and his war effort is waning. Half the soldiers are deserting. The Casualties are in the millions. Citizens are demanding that the Tsar step down. Many people in Petrograd are on the brink of starvation. There are shortages of fuel-oil and people are burning their furniture to stay warm.

I am thanking God I have the opportunity for a better life. Fortune has blessed me with a means of escape. With the savings from my acting career, I have purchased a billet on the steamship heading for Liverpool and hopefully to America from there. Nevsky Farce is moving the company to New York City. I am offered a part as a character actress. If my plans work out, I will send for you. But, Krystyna, right now I am bidding you a good night. I will continue later.

As ever and always,
Your loving mother

Despite the cold, beads of sweat wet Krystyna's forehead. Her heart jumped into her throat as reality breaks through. *"My family is in great peril. I must return to them at once. I never should have left them".* In a state of panic, Krystyna quickly gathers her meager belongings and hastily pens a note to her mother. Stuffing the journal and a loaf of bread into her satchel, she enters the dark, bitter cold streets of Petrograd and begins a lonely walk towards the train station.

Chapter 13

Hoping for cheese, bread, or milk, the proletariat form stationary lines outside shuttered storefronts. Warming fires encircled by desperate humanity dot Nevsky Prospect as Krystyna hurries by. Suddenly an old woman steps in her path. "Dear lady, please, my grandchildren and I have been out here for days with nothing to eat. There is no more wood to keep our fire burning. We are begging for your help."

"Here's half a loaf. That is all that I can spare. I'm hungry too." Krystyna hurries away. Suddenly she stops, retraces her steps. "Here, feed the children with the rest of this loaf. And warm yourselves with these papers. The blaze makes visible the woman's tears. "Don't despair. Better days must be coming," Krystyna advises.

"May the Lord reward your kindness, my lady." Wiping away a tear,

Krystyna quickens her pace past darkened doorways. *Click*—a flash of light and the smell of burning tobacco. Krystyna moves away from the buildings, into the street. A shadow is following her. She feels a vise grip and a tug on her arm that spins her around. The glowing streetlight reveals Sergei's hard features.

"You followed me here," shouts Krystyna.

"Not exactly. I have other business."

Krystyna shivered violently. "Are you stalking me? What is this business?"

"The motherland is more in danger from its citizens than from Germany." I'm here to protect the Tsar and his family. I've gone underground."

" And what do you want from me?"

"I want your hand in marriage."

Krystyna looks away. "That's impossible, at times like this. Besides, you know of my feelings for Tomasz."

Sergei lights another cigarette. "This is no place to talk." Krystyna feels the grip again on the back of her elbow, directing her towards the buildings. "I can help you find shelter in the Winter Palace."

"What? The Winter Palace? I can't stay in Petrograd. My family may be in danger from the Bolsheviks."

"I fully understand. But you need a plan. You've been running for too long. How's that working out for you?"

"Where are you taking me?

" The Tsar's Palace. I'm with the Secret Guard. You can be a housekeeper. You'll be training until spring."

"I can't wait 'til spring."

"Did you meet your mother?"

"Yes, fate did allow it."

"I thought so because I've seen a change in you."

"We didn't have much time to talk. My fault really. I had bad dreams about my family on the estate. I belong back home."

"I'll get you a passport and train ticket. I'd go with you if I could. Maybe after this chaos is over."

"Do you know Tomasz' whereabouts."

"He's back at the front."

"The front?"

"Wasn't cut out to be a medic."

"You-you sent him."

"Higher-ups make those decisions," he said with a shiver.

Sergei moves down Nevsky Prospect away from the train station. They pass office buildings, two foreign hotels, and finally they reach the Winter Palace overlooking the frozen Neva River. Flashing credentials, he escorts Krystyna to a back entrance. "Meet

Danuta. She will show you your quarters and begin the orientation. I will be checking on you daily. Do not leave the Palace without permission. Goodbye for now."

"Sergei, I am overwhelmed with emotions. I don't know what I think or feel. But good night, Captain."

Danuta pulls her through the doorway. "I am glad to meet you, Krystyna. I also am from Old Poland, the district of Galicia which is now Ukraine. First, be very careful about what you say in front of Sergei. He looks at everyone as a potential revolutionary. Tomorrow you will see how lavishly the Romanov's live, while you yourself will feast off the scraps that fall from their table."

"I see now why my mother moved here. There is a chilly, haunting beauty here on a scale I never imagined possible. Frankly, I don't understand why the Romanov's call it the Winter

Palace. That just reinforces the cold and darkness. Is it safe for me to speak to you this way?

"You can trust me with just about any secret."

"I need your help. My mother lives on the top floor of the Singer building, very close to here. I need to see her when possible. She is hungry like everyone in Petrograd."

"I would have to smuggle you out. You can leave, disguised as me. I will tell you when it is safe. You can take some food if you are discreet."

"Danuta, you must not put yourself at risk. I can taste nothing but tension and discontent. Ingredients for a fiery explosion. My nerves are on edge."

"For good reason. Don't worry about me. I will slip out early to join a bread line. But I have spare peasant garb, yours to borrow. Wrap the wool babushka around your face and tuck the fur cap tightly over it. Do not make eye contact with anyone. Get a good night's sleep."

"I don't know how to repay your kindness. But I have one more request of you."

"What is it Krystyna?"

"Do not unlock the door," Krystyna cries in a sudden, shaky voice. She grabs a wooden kitchen chair, jamming it under the doorknob. Her body shakes violently as she collapses into Danusha's arms. She tries to speak to no avail. Danusha sits her in the chair and mobs her brow with a wet towel. "The meeting with my mother was disastrous. And then the news about my dear Tomasz. If anything happens to him, Sergei be damned. Another strange encounter with him. What do you know about him. He is such a bully. But twice now he has saved my life. I had no plans when I ran from my mother. But here I am, in the palace of the Romanovs, of all places. I can't be alone tonight. May I stay with you?"

"Of course, and tomorrow you will see your mother if you wish. Yes, Sergei is a very strange man. Mentally unstable, I believe. If he does something for you, he thinks he owns you. He demands total loyalty. Be very careful."

Chapter 14

Krystyna spends half the night thinking about the Royal Family in the quarters below them. Could Tsarina Alexandra persuade her five children that they were safe? Is there any way to make sense of the assassination of their friend, Father Grigori? Would Tsar Nicolas II return from the front to protect them?

Her thoughts then return to her own family. Would they find safety from the peasant uprising? How was she going to explain her bad behavior to her mother tomorrow? Then Janina came to mind. *I wonder if she knows of the assassination. Did the Bolsheviks plan it? I must write to her directly.*

The next morning, she rides the elevator to the sixth floor of the Singer building. The doors part, giving Krystyna a grand view of the Winter Palace. The frosted windows blur her vision of mounted Cossack troops patrolling Palace Square and the river embankment. Her heart skips a beat at the sight of armed police officers surveilling the crowds from the rooftop of the Winter Palace and other buildings along Nevsky Prospect.

Krystyna's stomach flutters as she approaches her mother's apartment. She raps gently. Tanya opens the door wide, enveloping Krystyna in her arms. "Thank God you are safe. I've been praying since you left. We have so much to talk about. Her sobbing mother collapses in a chair and Krystyna eases to the floor, resting her head on her lap. "Mother, I need you and you are leaving for America. How can this be happening? Running from us again?"

Tanya strokes her daughter's hair. "A door has opened. I cannot allow this opportunity to escape. But you are in my plans."

"My home is here. I have family here and, besides, I may be in love."

"I don't expect you to understand. Who is the boy of whom you speak?"

"A Russian soldier, now on the Eastern front. The war casualties are escalating. My stomach churns when I think of him. He is from Vilnius. Raised in a Polish orphanage. He's been told his parents were Jewish." Krystyna sees blood drain from her mother's face. "I'm not too sure about that because he has blond hair and the most gorgeous blue bedroom eyes."

"Jewish? God forbid." Tanya crosses herself three times, in the Orthodox tradition, and continues. "Orthodox or Catholic?

"Catholic by practice. He is kind, protective, humble, and brave. All qualities I admire."

"Those bedroom eyes will only take you so far. But I'm so happy for you."

"Mother, when does your ship sail for England. Your departure will cancel my reason for being here. It's risky being here. I'm on house arrest and sightseeing is out of the question. Safe for now if I do what they say. I will leave as soon as I get a chance. Beautiful as this city is, it has lost its appeal. Are we witnessing an insurrection or a revolution?"

"I can't answer that. That's why I must leave. I have no definite date, but it will be after Christmas."

"Strike up the samovar. I brought some black bread and cheese."

Suddenly there is a loud knock on the door. "Police. Open up."

Two tall, slender men in black leather greatcoats push their way in. "Krystyna Karecki, you are under arrest. And Mrs. Karecki, show your visa. Our intelligence shows you are emigrating to America with the Russian Comedy troupe in January. I have seen your performance. Quite hilarious."

"Sir, what are the charges?" Krystyna asks.

"You are a suspected socialist and communist sympathizer. You left the Palace without credentials. By order of Captain Chukovsky, you have lost all privileges at the Winter Palace. Furthermore, you are assigned to the Anglo-Russian Hospital on Nevsky Prospect where your nursing skills are needed. You will live and work at the hospital for three months under house arrest. This may be the last time you see your mother. Finish your tea and say goodbye."

"As you wish. But I travelled 400 miles to be with my mother for Christmas."

"Save your sentimental reasoning for someone who cares," barked the tall dark figure. Grabbing the teacup, he hurls it across the room. "You're finished,"

Tanya smothered her daughter with hugs and eased her towards the door. She whispered,

"Do what they tell you. Your survival depends on clear thinking."

"Yes, mother. Bon voyage. A great adventure awaits you in the United States."

The Russians pulled the duo apart, slamming the door in Tanya's face. "Listen Carefully. Go directly to the Winter Palace and gather your things. Meet your hospital supervisor at 1 PM. Be aware, we are watching your every move."

Krystyna exits the elevator and is greeted by stiff chilling wind as the doorman pushes open the heavy glass door. The cold finds every gap in her fur coat, muffle, and gloves. She's greeted at the back entrance by a figure in black.

"Krystyna, let me help you with the door."

"I'd rather not see or speak to you, Sergei."

"Things are not what they appear, my dear."

"Your behavior is abusive and vindictive. Breaking your promises, kicking me out before I have even seen this magnificent palace or even laid eyes on the Imperial family. And now I'm told I can't see my mother."

"House arrest is for your safety, Krystyna. Demonstrations on the streets are intensifying. The Tsar has ordered the army to fire on the crowds to disperse them if necessary."

"How can I trust you. You are charging me with subversion and treason. What delusional and paranoid thinking."

"I am not lying. There are soldiers on the roofs of buildings all along Nevsky Prospect. You can see them

146

from here. They are equipped with machine guns which you cannot see. Our informers tell us the socialists will disturb the peace. The twelfth anniversary of Bloody Sunday is approaching and International Women's Day is February 23rd. The women are tired of standing in sub-freezing weather from five AM for bread. People are dying from hypothermia."

"Sergei, everyone in Petersburg is war-weary, cold, and hungry. And now you'll have me deal with blood, rotting flesh, human misery again. I can't do it."

"The need is real and you have proven your competence."

"I'm also competent at housekeeping."

"The doctors have been asking for you. Could you do it for the Motherland? Krystyna, when this is all over, we can start a family."

"Sergei, your promise rings hollow. You put me on house arrest, assign me to hospital work, and you except loyalty to Holy Russia and support for the Tsar? He is doing a terrible job and he should step down."

"He is a holy man and I will protect him with my life."

"Only a saint or Jesus Christ himself could forgive him for ordering the Imperial Guard to fire on peaceful protestors on that Sunday in 1905, religious procession disrupted by nervous soldiers. Nicolas may be an excellent father to four beautiful daughters and a sickly son, but he is lamb in a lion's den and he misuses his power in violent and unjust ways. He is blind to the needs and sentiments of the people."

"I disagree with your comments. Women should stay out of politics, No one is perfect. We all make mistakes."

"Some are costlier than others."

"Russia cannot exist without a supreme leader and we have one appointed by God. Those who oppose him will suffer dearly."

"Are conditions any better for the people since his coronation? No social reform in twelve years, except now the bread of the peasants and workers feeds the army. Will the Imperial Guard fire on the striking workers again?"

"The soldiers must follow orders or be executed."

"Your words pierce my heart. Whose blood will be on the streets? Are you trying to prepare me for the worse?"

The hospitals must be ready for whatever happens," Sergei reminds her. "I will do what I can to provide you with an opportunity to spend Christmas Day with your mother."

A month later

The bitter cold holiday season in Petrograd continued into January and February chilling festive spirits. Days disappeared without Krystyna seeing her mother. Wind chills reached -20 F, discouraging planned street demonstrations near the Winter Palace.

In mid-February Krystyna receives a visit from Danusha, her friend from the housekeeping department of the Winter Palace. "Krystyna, this letter came for you. I believe it is from Riga."

"This is unexpected. I hope to receive only good news. Danusha, I am deeply grateful for all you have done for me. This letter is precious to me. Give me a moment. This maybe important."

"Of course, my dear."

Her hands tremble as she slits open the letter with care.

Krystyna Karecki
Housekeeping Department
Imperial Winter Palace
Petrograd, Russia
January 15, 1917

My Dearest Krystyna,

I am overjoyed to receive your letter and to know by the powerful grace of God that you are safe. I'm profoundly grateful that our friendship endures despite my bad behavior. There is no excuse for my action upon your departure. With your forgiveness, all will be well. I will love you always.

I have exciting news for you. Mother Faustina and I are coming to Petrograd on the 23rd of February. We will participate in the International Women's Day to protest food shortages and unjust labor practices in urban Russia. Mother will not be in her habit and she is quite nervous about this. You and I know how resilient and adaptable she is. Pray there will be a break in the weather.

We have reservations at the woman's boarding house. Please advise us how to keep in touch. I look forward to seeing you after all these months.

Your dearest friend,
Janina Ostrowski

*** *

Krystyna gasps in disbelief. *Do they know the present danger. How can I warn them. I must telegraph them immediately.* She paces the rooms like a nervous puppy looking for its master. Finally, she settles down at the desk and dips the quill into the ink well. After several attempts she composes the following:

Janina,
Come alone to the Russian-Anglo Hospital.

Do not tell anyone you know me. Just say you are a volunteer sent by the Red Cross.
Krystyna

***

"Danusha, we need to talk before you take this letter to the telegraph office."

"I see your nerves are on edge. Mine are too since the assassination of Rasputin."

"The word on the street is that he was killed because he was promoting peace and an early withdrawal of Russia from the Great War against Germany and her allies."

"The talk all over Petersburg is that Tsarina Alexandra should be the next target due to her sympathies towards Germany. They are also calling for Tsar Nicolas to step down due to a series of blunders, including his choice of a German for Empress."

"If the revolutionaries can convince the peasants and idle urban workers to turn their rifles on the ruling class, Russia will be turned upside down.

Chapter 15

Krystyna, her coworkers, and ambulatory patients have a bird's eye view of demonstrations on Nevsky Prospect. The demonstration to commemorate Bloody Sunday stayed peaceful, mainly because most of the socialist agitators and reformers stay off the wind-swept streets. The massacre's two hundred victims were honored and remembered through a religious procession following the original route, from Kazan Cathedral to the gates of the Winter Palace. Except this time the demonstrators carried no demand for human rights because they knew the Tsar was not at home. It remained a religious procession. But a break in the weather was about to spark a revolution.

February 21, 1918 – Petrograd, Russia

"Nurse Karecki, there is a volunteer downstairs without Red Cross credentials. Could you please begin the paperwork?"

"Of course, Nurse Supervisor."

To Janina, she whispers, "Act like you don't recognize me. I can hardly stop myself from smothering you with hugs and kisses. When it is safe, we will go to the British Embassy to have your paperwork notarized. I am not permitted to leave the Hospital, but we will risk it when the time is right. I am being watched by the secret police but they are so involved with controlling the angry mobs that I may be able to move on the streets unnoticed. But our time is limited."

"Krystyna, I am here to beg you to return with us to Riga when the Women's Day March is over."

"I am ready, but travel is restricted due to the war. I have been offered safe passage out of Petrograd by an officer who I helped nursed back to health. The only problem is he insists on privileges. I refuse to compromise my morals."

"There is another way out of here, but it is shrouded in secrecy for now."

"How dreadful that we cannot speak freely. With haste let us take leave. I am so excited to see Mother Faustina."

"The journey will take a half hour, partly by tram and partly by foot. She's resting in the boarding house. She very much wants to march in solidarity with the women tomorrow and she's delighted by the prospect of seeing you as well."

The streets are already crowded with protesters. Some are waving red flags. Others carry banners which read, "Bread, Peace, Land".

"The Bolsheviks want the Duma to end the war. This will allow peasant soldiers to return to their farms. Russia would be able to feed its people again. Land reform will come by wiping away the bourgeoisie and the churches, so the land can be distributed to whoever wants to work it," explains Krystyna.

"The radical liberals will promote the revolution by any means necessary. They will need the military to join their side. Their agenda is too radical in my opinion," responds Janina.

"Janina, I agree." The pair lock arms and wind their way through melting snow to reach the boarding house. "May I visit with Mother privately. I'm so excited to see her and I have something personal to give her."

"Of course. I believe she would love that also. Here she comes to greet us."

"Oh Mother," exclaimed Krystyna." How strange to see you without your Holy Habit. How are you feeling?"

"It is only as "Holy" as the person wearing it. Sometimes it's comfortable to wear and sometimes not so much. Don't get me wrong. I love my habit but this feels like a break."

"You girls have so much to talk about. Let's go inside where we will be more comfortable."

They enter the foul-smelling hallway and meet in Mother's room.

"Mother, I'm returning the crucifix, once stained with blood. I believe it saved my life."

"My precious, tell me about your adventures when you have time. What is the mood on the streets?"

"As tight as a bride's girdle. People are calling for an end to autocracy. With Rasputin gone, the Tsar seems more vulnerable. The soldiers are tense, but friendly. Rasputin's assassins are cheered like heroes. People want change."

"I will be carrying an icon of Our Lady of Częstochowa while praying the rosary for peace tomorrow," Mother says. "And the crucifix will be around my neck. But I have something of grave importance to tell you. Sit down and take three deep breaths. The news is that your father is in Petrograd. He and his servant are looking for lodging in another part of town. You will see him soon."

"What? He really hates to travel. Ever since being injured in the Crimean war."

"There's more, Krystyna. He brought us here. The truth is, he and I have been writing letters since the move to Riga. He knew he couldn't stop you from pursuing your mother, but when word reached the countryside about the assassination, he understood the danger of riot in Petrograd. He came to Riga and begged me to join his mission to get you back home."

160

"I will return with you if I can escape my arrest, but I doubt my father will even speak to me again."

"You may be surprised. He may try to kidnap you."

"Mother, I do not want you and Janina to be caught in a revolution. I want to leave as soon as possible, but I am under heavy surveillance, so let me return to the hospital."

"Yes, I understand. Here is your diploma. Congratulations."

"Thank you. I hope I can put it to good use in the new Russia. Janina, Mother is wise to give you teaching position."

Krystyna returns unnoticed to the hospital.

***

The next morning Mother and Janina wake up, covered with flea bites. They greet the sun and cloudless sky. The air is a pleasant 20-degree

161

Fahrenheit. "Old lady, you can't carry that icon. This is not 1905, and this is not a religious procession," yells a socialite agitator. "Bread for the people and an end to the war," another man shouts from his soap box. "Seize that foreign object. There is no place for religious sentiment that doesn't feed the people."

"Stop", screams Janina. "Leave my mother alone."

"I am not comfortable with this. Holy Spirit guide me. I want everyone to be safe. And a positive outcome for the demonstrations. But you go on. I suppose I am quite naive regarding the ways of the world. But Janina, continue if you like."

"I feel strongly for other people and I would like to go on."

"Then I will see you in the afternoon."

Women lead the protests on February 23, International Women's

Day. Their cause is supported by the Duma who decry the bread shortages and labor conditions. The parade organizers are ladies from Petrograd's high society, female students, and urban peasants. In the afternoon female textile workers from across the Neva River go on strike and join their oppressed sisters. They are blocked by the police, but take a detour, crossing the river on thinning ice. The Cossacks, usually a strong fighting force, try to disperse the crowd but are unsuccessful. This emboldens the crowd. By the end of the day the women have a sense that they have started the revolution, over a shortage of bread and herring for themselves and their hungry children. Demanding better working conditions, the striking workers, numbering in the hundreds of thousands, swell the streets of Nevsky Prospect, increasing the tension with police and imperial guards, especially when the women break into shops and help themselves to bread and cakes.

Meanwhile Mother Faustina's prayer is interrupted by a knock at the door.

"Come in, Czeslaw. The girls are out on the march. It is safe for us to talk."

"Reverend Mother, I am so grateful you are part of the plot to get Krystyna out of this hotbed of political intrigue before the lid blows off."

"I have talked with her and she's ready to return with us to Riga or the estate. She misses her brothers as well."

"So, we don't have to kidnap her?"

"Not at all."

"Did she find her mother?"

"I don't know. We didn't have time to talk about it."

"Okay, I am just concerned about her attitude towards me. If she's ready to talk."

"What is it, seven months since you've talked? I think she's ready."

"Well, the plan is to return by the same route we took. My double-skid troika sleigh worked brilliantly on the way here. If the weather holds, we should be able to cover 300 miles to Riga in three or four days.

"Let's hope we have decent weather. And a decent place to stay."

"Mother, this is Russia, the peasants will welcome us if there is a snowstorm."

"I trust you. I don't know the ways of the world. I wanted so much to be part of the march, but I knew we had to meet. The icon served its purpose. Now I'm ready to take to the streets."

"There must be a hundred thousand women and strikers out there. Impossible to meet the girls, but let's go see what's going on."

The pair try to catch up with the marchers. Krystyna and Mother meet up with the striking workers. What are you marching for?" the young girl asks. "Dignity, respect, and better working conditions in that order", replies the agitator with the bullhorn.

"Explain please."

"We are not treated like human beings by management. They act like they own us. It's mental serfdom. They don't care if we eat, sleep, or fart. The only weapon we have is group solidarity and strikes. We demand an eight-hour work week, and better wages. But right now, we are supporting the women in their demand for bread."

The next day, soldiers defy their officers commands to fire on the crowd. "This mob is only asking for bread," they shout.

"This is mutiny. This whole regiment will face court martial," shouts a highly decorated senior officer.

"Go to hell," replies a soldier who is immediately slashed across the neck.

Gunfire breaks out and the officer falls to the pavement.

Soldiers shoot in the air to satisfy their officers. This defiance emboldens the crowd to louder protests. Soon, however, machine guns, manned by the police, appeared on rooftops.

Krystyna watches in horror from the second-story dayroom as the crowd turns violent. Agitators smash shop windows looking for bread. The police opened fire, painting the new snow crimson red. She watches in terror. She clutches her stomach and lets out a shriek when she recognizes the dark-haired figure in full dress uniform riding into the crowd with his saber drawn. The mounted Cossacks of the Imperial Guard are a few paces behind him. At his command they draw their sabers. The sound of steel reverberating against steel makes an ominous sound and silences the crowd. Captain Sergei's path is soon blocked by an angry mob that presses on him. A teenager, boosted by companions, jumps Captain Sergei from behind and throws him from his horse. Protesters plummet his head and face with bottles and a woman scratch at his eyes. A student wrestles the saber from him and slices deeply into his arm before he can draw his revolver. Krystyna pushes through the crowd with a stretcher balanced on her head. "Make way. Don't kill him. Have mercy on his poor soul." The crowd continues its march on the Palace, smiling and laughing with the Cossacks who cheer them on. Krystyna cradles Sergei's head in her lap and cries for help. Two boys take up the stretcher and move the victim towards the hospital, ignoring the murderous talk by the crowd. "He's with the secret police. He doesn't deserve to live."

Krystyna finds him a bed, stitches up his arm and nurses his facial wounds. She returns to his bedside with a shot of vodka. Then she hears him moaning, "You saved my life."

She wipes tears from her eyes, clasping his strong hand with both of hers. Their eyes meet and he falls back to sleep. Later that night she is awakened from slumber by shattering glass. As she enters the hospital ward, she hears a single gunshot. She charges at the dark figure standing over the Captain's bed. He raises a smoking revolver at her. She covers her face and slumps to the floor when she recognizes him as the perpetrator who assaulted her at Riga. Not recognizing her, he retraces his steps and exits the hospital. She blots the blood from the fresh gunshot wound but cannot stop the bleeding. Krystyna's body shakes uncontrollably, and her skin breaks out into hives. She lies on the floor until another dark figure picks up her head and applies a wet compress to her forehead. She awakes to the sensation of being carried. "I have you now sweetheart. All will be well," whispers Czeslaw as he lays Krystyna in her bed. "You are leaving here as soon as you are able. I'm taking you to the boarding house where Mother and Janina will care for you."

"Anatoly is downstairs, and he will carry you all the way."

"Anatoly is here in Petrograd. I don't understand."

"You don't need to. It will become clear in time."

"I must gather my things and change my clothes."

"Get some rest first. I'll explain the plan to the nurse supervisor. I think you will need something to help you sleep. You must be fully recovered before we travel. The weather can change in a heartbeat and cause frostbite or hypothermia."

"I trust you *Tata*, but I doubt I can sleep before I see Anatoly."

"Rest now. I'll take care of it," says Czeslaw as he tucks Krystyna in bed.

Czeslaw moves to a window and surveys the scene below. Rumor and debates are circulating about the mysterious, brave but foolish, nurse who saved the life of a gallant senior officer who attacked demonstrators. "Officers like him sent us into battles we could not win. We need peace and we need it now. The Duma denounces the food shortages but not the war. I am a peasant warrior and I support the Bolsheviks because they want to end the war with Germany. Damn that nurse."

Czeslaw makes eye contact with Anatoly and gestures for him to come up. As they pass through the crime scene, Anatoly spits on the corpse and makes an obscene gesture. He hurries to his love interest's bedside but freezes at the sight of all her cuts and bruises,

"I am too weak and exhausted to move now, but maybe in the morning. I'm glad you are here and will accompany us to Riga. I feel safe when you are around,"

"It is my pleasure, my lady. You have been in my constant thoughts since the day you left the estate."

"Enough of that. We will talk at another time". She raises her arms and lifts her head off the pillow. He hugs her and kisses her cheeks. "Please get some sleep. I think we can leave behind this chaos tomorrow." He bows profoundly from the waist, clicks his heels, and exits the building.

The next morning Czeslaw enters the room and wraps Krystyna in a blanket and hands her to the outstretched arms of Anatoly who slings her over his shoulder. Czeslaw grabs her. They exit the hospital undetected. "Hug the buildings and move as fast as you can," instructs Czeslaw. "There are machine guns on the rooftops and we are violating the curfew like everyone else." They scurry past the secret police loading Sergei's body into a flatbed truck.

They returned to the flea-bitten boarding house where Mother Faustina and Janina Ostrowski care for Krystyna. The next morning Anatoly professes his love for her and describes the pain he experienced in being separated from her. Her safety is his everyday worry.

"Anatoly there can be no future between us. I cannot explain it now, but some day in the future I will."

"I cannot bear the news. My heart and my whole body are trembling. But rest now. We will leave for home as soon as the snow flies again. With the troika sleigh and our three horses we can reach Riga in three days."

Krystyna is confined to her bed for the remainder of the February Revolution. In all, some 1300 souls are lost in the streets of Petrograd. While on their escape from Petrograd, Anatoly, the coachman, and his four passengers learn that Emperor Nicolas II abdicates the throne, thus ending 300 years of the Romanov dynasty. The country is in chaos. The power vacuum is in the hands of a provincial government influenced by socialist revolutionaries. The empire is unrecognizable to the former tsar and autocrat of all the Russias. He, along with his family, are on house arrest at their mansion some 30 miles from Petrograd.

In early March snow flew and the weather turned cold again. Czeslaw and Anatoly pack the sleigh with bear-skin blankets and sable caps and mufflers and cross town to pick up their three passengers. The icy wind picked up as Anatoly whipped the horses to 35 mph over the open steppe. He gives the horses free rein and keeps the sleigh gliding in a straight line across the frozen tundra and blinding snow. They will reach Riga in three and a half days.

One evening Krystyna is startled by a strong rap at her bedroom door. She cracks open the door to see a disheveled figure with dirty blond hair pulled back in a ponytail. His facial features are distorted by dim light and a thick beard. "Bang," she slams the door and bolts it. She takes a minute to ponder who the somewhat familiar figure might be. "Tanya, open the door. It's me."

"Tomasz, I almost gave up hope of seeing you alive. Come in and wash your face and hands. Tell me how you escaped the war."

"Our trenches came under enemy artillery fire. My left ankle was pierced by shrapnel. I have a festering wound which will not heal."

"Let me look at it. Here, prop your foot on this nightstand." Krystyna unwraps the moist, discolored rag. "Mercy. When did you last change the pad? That gash is to the bone. A laceration like this one should have been stitched together immediately. It's putrefied and must be treated every other day. If you wish to save your leg, you must stay here six weeks or more so I can treat it."

"You are my last hope. Your goodness brought me here. I will try to be a compliant patient."

"Good. Let me seek Mother Faustina's approval for use of the guest room. I certainly will welcome your company."

"We will continue were we left off seven months ago."

Krystyna felt blood rushing to her face, causing her to blush. "Much remains to be seen. Time is the best medicine."

***

Later that day, while Krystyna was doing laundry, Anatoly appeared in the courtyard. "It is urgent that we talk," he said. "I see strange men entering the building. I need to know where I stand in your life."

Dropping her basket of wet towels, she grabbed both his wrists and directed him to a shady bench and sat down in front of him. "This conversation will not be easy. Certain people have been keeping secrets from you for a very long time. As a result, we must take a different path."

On his feet now, he yelled, "What could it be? I will kill anybody who gets in our way."

"Sit down, take a deep breath, and I will tell you what I know. Anatoly, you were adopted as a toddler. While I was in Petrograd, I learned that Czeslaw is your father and Irina is your mother."

"I don't believe it. How false can people be."

"I have had time to absorb it. I suggest you go back to the farm and think things through."

"So, we are brother and sister. What a cruel joke. I am heartbroken and I will leave as soon as I can. Did he admit to it?"

"Yes, according to my mother."

"Damn him. I detest him and I'll never speak to him again." He covered his face to hide his emotions and walked away without saying goodbye.

***

"Can I come in?" Krystyna asked Janina late at night.

"I am awake now, so come on in. What's on your mind "

"That was one of the hardest things I have ever done,"

"You mean meeting with Anatoly."

"Yes. Not only is he infuriated with me, but he also lost all respect for my father. Tomorrow he must drive Czeslaw some 200 miles to reach the estate. I have decided to stay here with Tomasz until he is able to travel.

Probably two months. In the meantime, you and I, and Mother Faustina and Tomasz must decide which political party we will back because the revolution is just heating up. Vladimir Lenin is ready to return from exile. He will use terror tactics to gain the upper hand on the Social Democrats. The Bolsheviks will execute their planned takeover by any means necessary."

"My father, as you will recall, is a Bolshevik. He advises that we stay out of politics during such an intense power struggle."

"Tomasz and I will help Mother Faustina feed the neighborhood."

"I will be teaching the girls the principles of social Justice."

"But Janina, what are your long-term plans? The crisis in Russia can't last forever."

"I plan to return to Vilnius. I have friends there and my Aunt Lucja will return someday. If my mother gains U S

179

citizenship I would like to join her there."

"Now you are making sense. You deserve to be happy. They say it is the land of opportunity. Many Polish bachelors live there."

"I hate the thought of you leaving in two months, but I'm grateful we are safe. Our friendship will forever bring joy, peace, and love into our lives."

"Yes, it is not all gloom and doom."

Chapter 16

By mid-June Tomasz's leg had healed and Krystyna was making plans to have him meet Czeslaw at the estate. "I am hopeful my father will approve of our engagement. I want no more lies and secrets between us."

"I have concerns about his reaction when he learns I am a deserter."

"Janina tells me that half of the Tsar's army has deserted since his abdication."

"How would she know?"

"Her father wrote. This is the propaganda the Bolsheviks are spreading. Lenin has taken control of the party. He is promoting strikes and demonstrations in Petrograd. His red banners read: Bread!!! Peace!!! Land!!! He is promising an end to food shortages, withdrawal of Russia from the World War, and abolition of private property and inequality."

"His message has appeal among the masses who are weary of the war with Germany. The peasants are turning their anger against landowners and the privileged aristocracy, and they detest the taste of stale black bread." "Lenin is not a pacifist. He knows he needs the military for a violent uprising. His success depends on his ability to substitute one enemy for another."

"We shall see how it all plays out."

***

In July (1917) Krystyna receives her father's permission to marry Tomasz. He adds, "I would advise you to think long and hard about it. The country is in total chaos and a profound transformation is taking place. Your mother had the right idea, get out while the getting is good."

About a month later reports of armed demonstrations by industrial workers and soldiers in Petrograd have everyone on edge. Alexander Kerensky takes charge of the unpopular Provisional Government and slaughters hundreds of demonstrators who want Russia to withdraw from the war. He issues an arrest warrant against Lenin, who escapes to Finland. In October the Red Guard of the Bolshevik Party is organized by Leon Trotsky. His soldiers seize control of Petrograd. Lenin returns to take leadership of the party. On October 26, the Bolsheviks storm the Winter Palace and kill or arrest members of the Provisional Government. Another *coup d'état*. Lenin knows holding power will not be easy. He turns the secret police into an instrument of terror. Dubbed Cheka or the "All-Russian Extraordinary Commission to Combat Counterrevolution, Speculation, and Sabotage." This terrorist organization is headed by the brutal Polish nobleman-turned-Bolshevik, Felix Dzerzhinsky.

The Bolsheviks are the minority party and unpopular with many Russians because of their ruthlessness. On November 12 elections to the Assembly of the People takes place. The Socialist Revolutionary Party wins the most seats while the Bolsheviks secures less than a quarter of the vote. However, they maintain power by harassment, intimidation, and brutality.

In January,1918 Lenin negotiates a cease-fire agreement between Russia and the Central Powers. The news is greeted with great jubilation on the streets of Petrograd and Moscow. Soldiers returning from the Eastern Front will form the core of Lenin's new Red Army.

On March 3, the Treaty of Brest-Litovsk is signed, extricating Russia from WWI but at a great price. The Baltic states, along with Ukraine, are ceded to Germany. On March 8, the

Bolsheviks change the party name to Russian Communist Party.

Lenin had plans to put the former Tsar on trial for war crimes and crimes against the people, but the counterrevolutionary White Army, whose goal was to restore the Romanov dynasty, was within thirty miles of finding Nicolas II and his family. On the night of July 16-17, Lenin orders the secret execution of Nicholas II, Tsarina Alexandra, their five children, and several of their personal servants. The "Red Terror" escalates a month later because Lenin is seriously wounded by a would-be assassin. The Cheka responds with mass arrests and executions of suspected "enemies of the state".

***

During the summer of 1918, the Karecki family were constantly harassed by the communists. The Bolsheviks claimed their land and property. They confiscated all firearms, horses, livestock, produce, and grain. "How are we supposed to live?" screams Konrad at the top of his lungs. He paces the floor and flips over tables in the dining room.

"Please, get hold of yourself," begs Igor. "You'll wake *Tata* from his sleep."

"At this point do you think I care." In a rage he scurries through the kitchen to the barn, knocking dishes to the floor on the way. Minutes later the barn is ablaze.

A few days later Konrad gives a counterrevolutionary speech at a town hall meeting. It is not well received by the peasants. He flees for his life. Days later he is found in the woods by a posse of Communists. He resists arrest. The revolutionaries tie him between two trees and shoot him in the back of his head.

Villagers bring the tragic news to Krystyna who is tending the vegetable garden. "Oh my God. It can't be true." Igor and Czeslaw are inconsolable when they hear the news. "We must find his body before the animals do," warns Krystyna.

"Igor and I will get right to it but give us some time to talk. To Igor he says, "Son, you will soon be the head of this household for I am in poor health. I was your age when I took over this estate. You must become a man overnight and help me make wise decisions. Our lives depend on this."

"I am ready Father. What is it you want me to do?"

"You must dig the grave. My body will not allow me to do it. Together we will find the body."

"We only have a few hours of sunlight left. I will hitch up the wagon. We need lanterns. I know his favorite place to camp out. Maybe that's where he is."

They find the body. Igor spends eight hours digging the grave. At daybreak Krystyna finds her brother snoring rhythmically underneath an army blanket. She saunters off and returns shortly with a bottle of vodka and two shot glasses. After a half-hour of solitary drinking, she dislodges his cocoon and asks, "Where are we going? What is our future?"

"I have no definite plan, but obviously we are not safe here. Can we stick together? I see no future for myself here in Russia. I want to go to a place that's more in step with the world. What about you?"

"For better or worse, this is my country, but I'm scared to death."

"To me, that is a sign you should leave."

"I'm in love with Tomasz."

"Fine, as long as you aren't fooling yourself."

"What do you mean?"

"Hidden anger. Have you forgiven mother? Maybe you are trying to prove how wrong she was. She could have stayed around. And what about *Tata*? All his drinking and pushing religion."

"I ought to knock you out with this bottle but not until it's empty."

"I'll drink to that."

"Damn. You give so a much to think about."

"Mercy me. That bottle is almost done."

Later that morning Konrad is interned near Stanislaw, his uncle Fr. Michael, and his grandfather Aleksander.

***

A few days later the grieving household are awakened by a volley of gunshots outside the front door. The four residents stagger down the grand staircase and shield their sleepy eyes from the blinding sun. "Search the premises for concealed weapons,

189

ammunition, jewelry, and other valuables," barks Comrade Anatoly Danilov, stableboy-turned-Cheka enforcer. The foursome quake in disbelief as they recognize the muscular figure mounted on a familiar black stallion. "Turn around, hands behind your back. On your knees." He dismounts, slaps each quivering detainee, starting with Irina, across the back of the head and pokes them with his smoking weapon. "You are now strangers to me, enemies of the State. You are under house arrest 'til further notice. My men will shoot anyone who tries to leave."

A dozen Red Guard soldiers appear, some carrying gold candelabras. One has a Fabergé baroque clock. "This is all we found." They circle the mansion a few times, then ride off, shouting, "Down with the bourgeoisie".

The four tremble as they enter the dining room. A letter from the revolutionary command raises further anxiety. Czeslaw reads it aloud.

SEPTEMBER 1, 1918
MR. C. KARECKI
PLISCHITSA DISTRICT ESTATE

PLISCHITSA DISTRICT LAND AUTHORITY ORDERS YOU TO VACATE THE ABOVE-MENTIONED ESTATE IMMEDIATELY (NO LATER THAN SEPTEMBER 4), AND TO MOVE NO LESS THAN 150 MILES AWAY. YOU AND FAMILY MEMBERS ARE NOT TO RETURN.

IN THE EVENT OF NON-COMPLIANCE WITH THIS ORDER, YOU WILL BE SUBJECT TO COURT PROCEEDINGS OF REVOLUTIONARY

SEVERITY. THIS ORDER IS
EFFECTIVE ON RECEIPT.

    SIGNED.

    F. I. ARTIZOV

    PLISCHITSA DISTRICT LAND
COMMISSIONER

***

"It appears the noose is tightening around our neck," remarks Krystyna.

"I want to leave Russia," says Czeslaw, wiping tears from his eyes. "I see only bitter suffering here for years to come. The liberated countries of Lithuania, Latvia, or Estonia are a safe haven."

"Latvia is the best choice," says Igor, "provided we can get past the German lines."

"Good thinking, my son. Most of the Germans have been redeployed to the Western Front. Plus, we are only ten miles from the border. We can get there on foot."

"I will be going in a different direction," says Krystyna. "Tomasz and I have plans to marry. I will take a train to Riga."

"My dear child, please consider your choices very carefully. These are not ordinary times. Can you live under Communism?"

"Whatever happens, I will put my trust in God."

"We will help you in any way we can," says Igor, turning and absorbing a smile from Irina.

"It's Latvia for the rest of us. I will pack all the documents proving land ownership, maps, deeds, family tree, contract agreements and the like. I hope the civil war will turn in favor of the White Army. But we must leave tonight. I do not trust these hot-headed revolutionaries."

"But father, you have a strong box with cement reinforcements on all six sides. Why don't you just bury all those items you want instead of taking everything with you. If the Whites are eventually successful as counterrevolution we could return to find and claim our buried treasure."

"My plan has more flexibility and safety. The civil war is far from decided. Who knows what the Reds will do. We don't know where the Tsar is. Some say he is dead. Some say the whole family was assassinated.
Perhaps they will construct buildings, or dig wells, or blow up the whole place. *'Ooh la la',* look what I found!' Who knows what the new Russia will look like."

"I bow to you father."
***

The trio make it into Latvia safely. Irina finds employment as a housekeeper but keeps in touch with

Czeslaw. Igor is motivated to finish his secondary education. He needs his father's help. After Church one Sunday they picnic together. "Son, I believe I will not live long. I suffer from emphysema and each day it gets harder for me to breathe. You, at age 16, have your whole life ahead of you. My son, go where you want to go. Do what you want to do."

"First, I must graduate."

"Excellent. We will find you a boarding school here in Daugavpils. Once you have your diploma, you will be on your own. I am really proud of you."

"My heart is full of joy and gratitude. But father, what about your plans?"

"Son, do not worry about me. I have friends who will take care of me."

Igor proves himself a serious student and easily makes friends. He embraces the Catholic faith and is

baptized. Early in his senior year he learns of his father's death. Traveling to Vilnius by train, he claims the body and fulfills his father's wish for burial at a Catholic cemetery overlooking the blue waters and white sandy shore of the Baltic Sea. He is unsuccessful in contacting his sister and her husband. According to friend Janina, they are involved with a soup kitchen somewhere in Moscow. Alone and anxious about his future, Igor seeks and finds a job as a cook/cabin boy on the *S.S. Latvia*, a passenger steam ship whose ports of call are Libau, Latvia and New York City. On his second voyage across the Atlantic, before the outcome of the civil war is known, he leaves the ship with German passengers and loses himself in the New World at the age of 19.
Someday I will find my mother, he tells himself.

The End

Epilogue

Igor stays with German friends he made on board the *S S Latvia.* They have a tiny apartment in lower Manhattan. He finds several odd jobs, such as dishwasher, short order cook, custodian. Eventually, he lands something more stable, namely, delivering new or repaired typewriters via the NYC Transit Authority (subway). This allows him to share an apartment with another Russian emigrant. Before long, he was promoted to typewriter repairs. He attends night school at the University and eventually obtains a degree in mechanical engineering. This opens the door to a career in the auto industry. Eventually he marries a Polish immigrant eleven years his junior. Before he can do this, he must find his mother, who will provide him with a path towards citizenship. With the help of his sister in Moscow he is united with his mother who has remarried. Her husband is a Russian clergyman living in Buffalo, NY. He is in his seventies and a recent widower, with several young children in need of mothering.

But first Tanya begs the Reverent for a trip to Soviet Russia to check on her daughter and her other relatives.

A visa is easy to obtain because she is a U S citizen and the Russian civil war is supposedly over. She stays with Krystyna and Tomasz in Moscow from March,1923 to June,1924. The couple have a one-year-old daughter, who is "the delight of their lives." Upon her return she reports to the FBI that terrorism is rampant and starvation is widespread amongst the peasants.

Krystan stays loyal to the government which, she feels, needs "more time" and citizen cooperation to implement their reforms." We will expand our vegetable garden and raise more chickens and goats," she says. Fortunately, fate smiles on Tomasz who discovers his aptitude for science and mathematics.   He becomes part of the team exploring electrification for rural Russia. He advocates for alternating current over direct current because he realizes that AC is far more efficient and practical. He delights in Nikola Tesla's victory over Thomas Edison's greed and fraud in the United Stated. He considers George Westinghouse his idol for righteousness.

***

Janina became a student assistant to her Aunt Lucja at Stephen Batory University in 1921. This was the new and temporary name of Vilnius University. In 1924, she receives a ticket to join her mother in Detroit, Michigan. She makes the Atlantic crossing alone. Unfortunately, her mother died of throat cancer shortly thereafter. Within a

199

matter of months, she attracts the attention of a handsome suitor of Polish descent. With the birth of her five children, Janina heals her lonely heart and achieves success in raising happy and independent children.

***

Mother Faustina resigned as superior of her convent. She takes the liberty to abandon her habit in favor of early morning bike rides on the eastern shore of the Baltic Sea. Her "new way of praying", she explains. One morning a high-flying seagull blinds her with its droppings. She falls onto the pavement, fracturing her hip. Surgical repair was successful but there are complications. On July 31,1920 Krystyna and Janina are at her bedside when she passes. She is buried by the Felician and Sulpician Sisters on a hill overlooking the Bay of Riga, the sight of the former orphanage destroyed by artillery fire from German Gunboats on September 1, 1918.

"In his own words"

We, his children, found Valerjan Kavetsky's handwritten notes after his death in 1988. Brief, but to the point, he describe his experience in Russia.

***

"I was born on June 29th, 1902, in Russia, formerly Poland. My father, Mieczyslaw, was the owner of 750 acres of land, which consisted of 250 acres of forest, 250 acres of a lake (Nitza), and 250 acres of meadows and cultivated land. In 1897 my father, a Catholic of Polish nationality, married my mother Tatiana, a Russian of the Orthodox religion. They had three children Tamara, Modest, and me, Valerjan.

Due to differences of religion and national origins. My parents could not agree on methods of baptizing and educating children. The Russian law required baptism in the Orthodox Church and forbid the teaching of Polish. My father ignored the law and hired private teachers to teach Polish. This created friction between my mother's family and my father. There was constant harassment of my father from law enforcement agencies and religious personnel. Finally, my mother left my father and went back to her relatives.

In 1911 she left for America with one of her distant relatives. My father filed for divorce but due to certain orthodox religious rules it was difficult to obtain.

In the fall of 1911, my father went to Riga, Latvia and enrolled the children in the Polish boarding school of Anna Zach. This was very expensive, so he rented an apartment. Tamara was still going to Zach School for Girls. The boys were transferred to public school.

Summer vacations were back on the farm.

In 1914 World War One broke out. Germans invaded Latvia. Our school was relocated to Velikie Luki. Russia, where we lived until 1917 when the revolution broke out. During summer vacations of 1918 we were constantly harassed by revolutionary communists who requisitioned our horses, livestock, grain, and guns. My brother Modest was executed by the mob for making a counter revolutionary speech at a county meeting. Next, we received a written order to leave the estate within three days and locate 150 miles from the German frontline in Latvia. Since the German line was only 10 miles away from our farm my father, me, and our housekeeper snuck through at nighttime to German occupied Latvia. Tamara got married and decided to stay in Russia."